THE CRAFT OF
AN ABSOLUTE
WINNER

Contributions in Afro-American and African Studies
Series Advisers: John W. Blassingame and Henry Louis Gates, Jr.

The Afro-Yankees
Providence's Black Community in the Antebellum Era
Robert J. Cottrol

A Case of Black and White:
Northern Volunteers and the Southern Freedom Summers, 1964-1965
Mary Aickin Rothschild

Gatekeepers of Black Culture:
Black-Owned Book Publishing in the United States, 1817-1981
Donald Franklin Joyce

MARIA LUISA NUNES

THE CRAFT OF AN ABSOLUTE WINNER

Characterization
and Narratology
in the Novels of
Machado de Assis

CONTRIBUTIONS IN AFRO-AMERICAN AND AFRICAN
STUDIES, NUMBER 71

Greenwood Press

Westport, Connecticut • London, England

Library of Congress Cataloging in Publication Data

Nunes, Maria Luisa.
  The craft of an absolute winner.

  (Contributions in Afro-American and African studies,
ISSN 0069-9624; no. 71)
  Bibliography: p.
  Includes index.
  1. Machado de Assis, 1839-1908—Characters. 2. Machado
de Assis, 1839-1908—Technique. I. Title. II. Series.
PQ9697.M18Z735 1983   869.3   82-11717
ISBN 0-313-23631-3 (lib. bdg.)

Library of Congress Catalog Card Number: 82-11717
ISBN: 0-313-23631-3
ISSN: 0069-9624

First published in 1983

Greenwood Press
A division of Congressional Information Service, Inc.
88 Post Road West
Westport, Connecticut 06881

Printed in the United States of America

10 9 8 7 6 5 4 3 2 1

Copyright Acknowledgments

Extracts from the following articles by Maria Luisa Nunes are reprinted, with changes,
by permission of the Latin American Literary Review:

"Machado de Assis's Theory of the Novel," LALR No. 7, Volume IV, Fall/
Winter 1975;

"Story Tellers and Character: Point of View in Machado de Assis's Last Five
Novels," LALR No. 12, Volume VI, Spring/Summer 1978;

"Allegory in Machado de Assis's *Esau and Jacob,*" LALR No. 21 or 22, forthcoming.

For Maria Da Luz
and
Edwin Leitão Nunes,
my parents

CONTENTS

PREFACE

JOAQUIM Maria Machado de Assis, 1839-1908, a mulatto, was Brazil's greatest prose fiction writer. Of humble origin, Machado de Assis was in large measure self-taught. During the liberal empire of nineteenth-century Brazil, color and class were not insurmountable obstacles as the success of many men of similar station and color attests. Machado de Assis rose from typographer to upper level civil servant with relative ease. According to the contemporary Brazilian critic Antonio Cândido, the only moment when his color seemed to be an impediment was when he married a white Portuguese. From all indications, her family objected to the match. Obviously, Machado de Assis's color meant little or nothing to his bride and the couple enjoyed a long and reportedly happy marriage. Machado de Assis counted among his friends many talented and distinguished Brazilians.

The Brazilian author was an extremely private person who led the quiet and somewhat regimented life of the civil servant and devoted the remainder of his time to his writing and to his wife. Understandably, his creations and his genius have elicited much speculation about Machado de Assis the man. Despite the many works that have delved into his life (see Introduction), the enigma of this man of genius remains unsolved. The character of Machado de Assis has been maligned and vindicated by the many people who have written about him. He emerges as quite a different person from the man of the legend. What becomes immediately apparent is that he was too subtle for his detractors. It is true that he was more concerned with the perfection of his art than with taking a militant role in social causes. Nevertheless, he took his stand on the issues and his perception of them was farsighted enough to comprehend more than their immediate implications. His art is a testimony to his success and fulfillment in his life's goal. He did not wish perhaps to be known as a black, white, or mulatto artist but as an artist. His concerns reflect a desire to be accepted in his unique identity, a desire common to all great artists and even to lesser human beings.

I am indebted to Yale University's Morse Fellowship for Junior Faculty, to the Radcliffe Institute for "a room of my own," and wish to express my thanks to Professors Paul de Man and Antonio Cândido and to Dr. Irwin Stern who read the entire manuscript and to Professors John Blassingame and Peter Demetz who read parts of it. Last but not least, I wish to thank the students at Yale for their collaboration in this book.

ABBREVIATIONS

FOR the initial research of this work, I consulted Machado de Assis's *Obra Completa*, organized by Afrânio Coutinho, Rio de Janeiro: Editora José Aguilar Ltda., 1962. For the purpose of facilitating references to the English translations, a list of their abbreviations as cited in the text follows. All the works except *Ressurreição* and *Helena* exist in published English translations.

R *Ressurreição. Obra Completa.* Organized by Afrânio Coutinho, Vol. I. Rio de Janeiro: Editora José Aguilar Ltda, 1962. (Translations my own.)

HG *A Mão e a Luva (The Hand and the Glove).* Tr. by Albert I. Bagby, Jr. Lexington, Kentucky: The University Press of Kentucky, 1970.

H *Helena.* Obra Completa. Organized by Afrânio Coutinho, Vol. I. Rio de Janeiro: Editora José Aguilar Ltda, 1962. (Translations my own.)

IG *Iáiá Garcia.* Tr. by Albert I. Bagby, Jr. Lexington, Kentucky: The University Press of Kentucky, 1977.

ESW   *Memórias Póstumas de Brás Cubas* (*Epitaph of a Small Winner*). Tr. by William L. Grossman. New York: The Noonday Press, 1952.

PD   *Quincas Borba* (*Philosopher or Dog?*) Tr. by Clotilde Wilson. New York: The Noonday Press, 1954.

DC   *Dom Casmurro.* Tr. by Helen Caldwell. Berkeley and Los Angeles: University of California Press, 1971.

EJ   *Esaú e Jacó* (*Esau & Jacob*). Tr. by Helen Caldwell. Berkeley and Los Angeles: University of California Press, 1966.

CAM   *Memorial de Aires* (*Counselor Ayres' Memorial*). Tr. by Helen Caldwell. Berkeley and Los Angeles: University of California Press, 1972.

THE CRAFT OF
AN ABSOLUTE
WINNER

1

INTRODUCTION

PREVIOUS CRITICISM

IN view of the very modern and original techniques employed by the Brazilian master, it is not surprising that many critics have been confused by his works and somewhat limited in their attempt to classify them. Oliveira Lima's speech at the Sorbonne, later published as *Machado de Assis Son Oeuvre Littéraire* (1917), is a eulogy to the Brazilian master focusing on the excellence of Machado de Assis's short stories, the links between his life and works, and his pessimism and irony. Among Machado de Assis's early critics, Alfredo Pujol (*Machado de Assis*, 2nd ed., 1934) demonstrated a certain preoccupation with classification when he asserted that Machado de Assis was a naturalist writer without the excessive crudeness of the school. Modestly, Pujol made no claims to being a literary critic, but in addition to establishing the legend of Machado de Assis's spectacular ascent from the depths of poverty to the heights of literary success, he pointed out Machado de Assis's philosophizing tendency. Another early critic, Alcides Maya (*Machado de Assis*, 2nd ed., 1942) noted

Machado de Assis's humor, philosophical bases, and pessimism, and placed him in a universal context of philosophy and literature drawing comparisons between the Brazilian master and Schlegel, Hegel, Hennequin, Scherer, Carlyle, Cervantes, Swift, and Sterne.

In a sense, the necessity of clinging to any simplistic label has probably obstructed recognition of the multifarious elements of Machado de Assis's artistry. The psycho-biographical approach that followed the early critics has been especially deficient in this respect. First of all, Machado de Assis's reticence about his personal life coupled with the vitality of his texts force the critic to deal with and analyze the texts themselves. Secondly, the psycho-biographical studies of the man and his works often verge on racism and contribute little to an understanding of the works. Their authors claimed that Machado de Assis's misanthropic and bitter attitude toward his fellow man and life as conveyed by his novels could be explained by his color, poverty-stricken background, stuttering, and epilepsy. Lucia Miguel Pereira was the first to apply this method (*Machado de Assis*, 1936). Although her criticism presents many interesting intuitions about Machado de Assis's art, her descriptions of him as "the stuttering mulatto," or the observation that "as a mulatto, he was unable to hide his race, screaming from the vast and rebellious head of hair falling over his ears, his thick lips covered by a stiff mustache under flattened nostrils," seem not only gratuitous but racist. Augusto Meyer's interpretation (*Machado de Assis*, 1958) is that of a subterranean man whose tedium of everything, hatred of, radical incapacity to accept or comprehend, and wish to suppress the world made him a critic and a destroyer. From this theoretical basis, Meyer analyzed the works. Mario Matos's *Machado de Assis* (1939) bears as its subtitle "The Man and the Works, the Characters Explain the Man." Matos proceeded to trace aspects of the author in the population of his fictional world. Eloy Pontes (*A Vida Contraditória de Machado de Assis*, 1939) is another critic whose method is to examine Machado de Assis's life with illustrations from his works. All Machado de Assis's idiosyncrasies are the stuff of his literary creations according to Pontes, who also touches on such points as the atmosphere of nineteenth-century Rio, Machado de Assis's attitudes as reflected by his chronicles, slavery in his works, his relationship to naturalism and Eça de Queiroz, and personal matters of taste. Pontes's conclusions, however, all relegate Machado de Assis to identification with his characters.

There are two critical curiosities that not very many people take seriously. Agrippino Grieco's *Machado de Assis* (2nd ed., 1960) purports to be an iconoclastic vision of Machado de Assis, which succeeds in presenting the reader with a reductionist, free-associative, gross, and gossipy work highlighted by the author's racial prejudice. At one point, Grieco wrote: "He (the narrator) refers to 'the immensely white color' of a young woman's skin, with a certain excitement of the grandson of Africans, but without vibrating the trembling lust that later, the daughters of Germans from Santa Catarina would arouse in the black, Cruz e Sousa." In the same sense, Afrânio Coutinho regales us in *A Filosofia de Machado de Assis e Outros Ensaios* (1940) with an eleven-page racist diatribe on the psychology of the mulatto, which in turn, is to assist us in understanding Machado de Assis's preference for the philosophy of Pascal.

Raymundo Magalhães's two books, *Machado de Assis Desconhecido* (3rd ed., 1957), and *Ao Redor de Machado de Assis* (1958), study less known writings of the Brazilian author and do a great deal to demystify the "black" legend around Machado de Assis, which asserted, among other things, that he was a traitor to other blacks and was not involved in the struggle for abolition. Josué Montello's *O Presidente Machado de Assis* (1961), also reveals unpublished materials on Machado de Assis including correspondence with his friends, his diary, and correspondence about the Brazilian Academy of Letters of which Machado de Assis was the first president. The definitive intellectual biography, as far as it goes, is Jean-Michel Massa's *A Juventude de Machado de Assis* (1971), which covers the years 1839-1870. It is a meticulously researched work that finally lays to rest much of the false information disseminated about the early life of Machado de Assis.

The premise that it is necessary to understand Machado de Assis's life in order to understand his works is false. The texts confront us with a brilliant originality that inspired itself from many sources, but ultimately produced a new and unique synthesis. Machado de Assis's inspiration ranged from the Bible to Homer, Aeschylus,

Xenophanes, Dante, Shakespeare, and Goethe, but the result of his art was his alone.

Beginning in the decade of the 1940s, Brazilian critics focused more directly on the texts. The work of José Barreto Filho, *Introdução a Machado de Assis* (1947), is the first genuinely astute criticism of Machado de Assis, and is scholarly and insightful. Barreto Filho avoids the pitfall of Machado de Assis's life as an explicator of his texts and leans toward a metaphysical interpretation of the works. Other esthetic criticism of Machado de Assis includes Eugênio Gomes's work, *As Influências Inglesas de Machado de Assis* (1939), which explores humor in Machadean texts and the influences of Shakespeare, Swift, Fielding, Sterne, Lamb, Thackeray, and Dickens. Gomes's *Machado de Assis* (1958) is a collection of essays that compare literature and the graphic arts, discuss the artist and society, give esthetic evaluations of nature, morality, and society, and discuss the role of naturalism and realism in Machado de Assis's art. Gomes also treats the origin of Machado de Assis's metaphors as well as the stylistic features of his works. His essay, "The Esthetic Testament of Machado de Assis," analyzes style, methodology, esthetics, and interprets allegory and philosophical influences.

There are a number of linguistic critical approaches including J. Mattoso Camara's *Ensaios Machadianos* (1962); Ivan Monteiro and Hairton Estrella's *A Metalinguagem em "Quincas Borba,"* an analysis of Machado de Assis's critique of the rhetoric, commonplaces, and pomp of the second reign in Brazil; and Maria Nazaré Lins Soares, *Machado de Assis e a Análise da Expressão* (1968), which is the most thorough and relevant of these studies in its contribution to an understanding of Machado de Assis's prose.

Other studies of a more modern flavor are Gustavo Corção's *O Desconcerto do Mundo*, which attempts to study Machado de Assis's creative rhythm, from analyzing his pessimism and skepticism to explaining his leap from mediocrity to greatness. José A. Castello's *Realidade e Ilusão em Machado de Assis* (1969), is an example of methodical research and an interpretation of the general sense or fundamental goals of Machado de Assis's work. Castello's quest to comprehend the artist's thought was based on a reading of a wide sample of his writings, including chronicles, criticism, poetry, and short stories. Dirce Cortes Riedel's *O Tempo no Romance Machadeano* (1959) and *Metáfora o Espelho de Machado de Assis* (1974), refer to contemporary categories and critics of esthetic theory such as Bakhtine, whose notions of the carnivalization of literature are well known, and provide the reader with new and interesting interpretations.

Astrojildo Pereira (*Machado de Assis*, 1959) analyzed society from his reading of Machado de Assis, directing his attention to the marriage of convenience, slavery, abolition, the Paraguayan War, the development of capitalism, political life, and the republic. Marxist criticism is the basis of Flávio Loureiro Chaves's *O Mundo Social de Quincas Borba* and involves a dialogue with previous critical texts such as those of Lucia Miguel Pereira and Antonio Candido. The most sophisticated Marxist criticism is that of Roberto Schwarz, *Ao Vencedor as Batatas* (1977), which is based on an economic analysis of paternalism during the second reign. The work treats only the first four novels of Machado de Assis and contrasts European romanticism as it existed in Brazil and Machado de Assis's transformation of it to a Brazilian realism. Schwarz analyzes possible relationships in the early novels under a system of paternalism and essentially gives to the reader an analysis of the society.

The sole North American critic, Helen Caldwell (*The Brazilian Othello of Machado de Assis*, 1960, and *Machado de Assis, the Brazilian Master and His Novels*, 1970), addressed herself to the texts, and analyzed them by means of intertextual readings with the works of Shakespeare, Sterne, and other classical authors. Caldwell's analysis of *Dom Casmurro* as a close kin of Shakespeare's *Othello* was one of the earliest critical works to focus on the narrator's jealousy as opposed to the Brazilian critical tradition of endlessly disputing Capitu's alleged adultery.

THE ART OF CHARACTER AND NARRATION

Machado de Assis produced nine novels between 1872 and 1908. Throughout these novels, he made comments on and observations about the art of imaginative literature. His texts reveal a set of directions for their fuller comprehension. He did not, however, leave an extensive body of letters and essays discussing his art and the development of his esthetic approach. Although he left to the reader the task of deciphering his literary program, his other writings—chronicles, literary criticism, poetry, and short stories—are additional sources for the critic of Machado de Assis's esthetics. Machado de Assis's critical advice to other writers can easily be interpreted as his own literary ideal.

During the period of Machado de Assis's novelistic production, romanticism was still flourishing but the incursions of naturalism were soon to be felt. In general, Brazilian romanticism is characterized by lyric poetry, indianism, poetry of the *mal du siècle*, and literature concerned with socio-political events such as abolition and the Paraguayan War (1865-1870). The movement included the expansion of literary genres, and was based on an exaltation of nature along with the observation and analysis of customs and characteristic types.[1]

From the beginning of his novelistic career, Machado de Assis outlined an experimental literary form which contained some romantic elements but was not strictly representative of the romantic novel. Certain statements made by Machado de Assis indicate that of the two prevailing schools of his time, he had a sentimental attachment to romanticism. While the earlier novels of Machado de Assis utilize a few romantic devices, it is clear that they demonstrate many of the features to be found in his later works. In breaking with the last features of the movement, marked by the publication of *Epitaph of a Small Winner* in 1881, Machado de Assis liberated himself not only from the school of Sir Walter Scott, but from all literary schools.

It was with particular virulence that Machado de Assis attacked the naturalist movement which he referred to as *realismo*. In his view, the naturalist poetics would only reach perfection when they could tell us the exact number of threads in a handkerchief or scouring pad. His advice to young writers in Portugal and Brazil was not to be seduced by a doctrine which, despite its novelty, was already obsolete. Although its influence could be good up to a point, it lacked the force of universality and vitality. It was not to be a substitute for accepted doctrines, and the excesses of its application had to be corrected. Machado de Assis urged looking toward reality but excluding naturalism. In this way, the esthetic truth would not be sacrificed. He was preoccupied as early as 1874 in his second novel, *The Hand and the Glove*, with the naturalness and truth of his characters.

Machado de Assis took from the reigning schools, romanticism and naturalism, only those elements which he was to make a peculiar part of his own esthetic. Although he confronted a public whose literary taste ranged from romanticism to naturalism and parnassianism, he persisted in following an autonomous route. That he would make no concessions to popular taste in literature is the fundamental point of departure he announced in *Epitaph of a Small Winner*, when he discussed the limited number of readers his work would have:

> That Stendhal should have confessed to have written one of his books for one hundred readers is shocking and appalling. What is not shocking and will probably not be appalling is if this other book does not have Stendhal's hundred readers, or fifty, or twenty, or even ten. Ten? Maybe five. [*ESW*, p. 17]

In the same paragraph, Machado de Assis outlined the technique of the work. He had adopted the free form of a Sterne or of a Xavier de Maistre with some sullen pessimism added. The fictionalized work of a dead man, Brás Cubas wrote the novel with the pen of mockery and the ink of melancholy. In *Epitaph of a Small Winner*, we first encounter the archaic techniques of eighteenth-century literature. Machado de Assis's archaism is surprisingly modern when we consider the tendencies of the avant garde. The whole is suggested by fragments, the structure by ellipsis, emotion by irony, and greatness by banality.[2]

As for his own works, Machado de Assis was somewhat cagey about explaining his processes. He is very much aware of them, however, and wants the reader to recognize them as well—while insisting that they are unnecessary to an understanding of the work which is all. He consistently appealed to and teased the reader as he outlined his literary goals. The artist has the power to restore the past, to touch upon the instability of our impressions, and the vanity of our affections. He wrote that each stage of life was like an edition of a book that improves on the previous one until the definitive edition which is given to the worms.

A more detailed examination of some of Machado de Assis's processes and techniques indicates that the most important element in his novels is character. What interested him above all was man. All of Machado de Assis's novels are determined by the conflicts of his characters' passions and temperaments. His ultimate esthetic aim for Brazilian literary art was to see the cultivation of the novel uniting the study of human passions to the delicate and original touches of poetry. In his view, this was the only way that a work of the imagination, oblivious to time, would reach the severe eyes of posterity pure and unaltered.[3]

If we continue our examination of Machado de Assis's processes and techniques, we find that those of characterization may be traced from theory to actual application. It must be remembered, however, that the body of Machado de Assis's work is divided into the earlier phase ending with the publication of *Iáiá Garcia* (1878), and the later phase marked by the publication of *Epitaph of a Small Winner* (1881). The theoretical bases of Machado de Assis's criticism differ in the two phases. In 1858, Machado de Assis advised the writers of the day to study society as a mine to be exploited. There, a talented writer could discover, copy, and analyze types and characters of all kinds.[4] From an admiration of romantic idealization, Machado de Assis followed a trajectory which took him through the advocacy of processes resembling naturalism to a parody of both schools in his character drawing.

The methods by which Machado de Assis implemented his character drawing were based on a keen sense of craftsmanship. The Brazilian author sought to dominate expression, refine his style, find the *mot juste*, and control the tumult of creation without losing spontaneity. He was always aware of excesses in composition.[5]

Related to Machado de Assis's highly developed sense of craftsmanship is the manipulation of satirical elements in his novels. In the Swiftian manner, Machado de Assis wished to chastize and indict society. The effectiveness of this exposure is a result of his craftsmanship. The Brazilian artist's use of the elliptic, the incomplete, the fragmentary, conversational interventions in the narrative, irony, and understatement is so elusive that often his readers are left perplexed as to his real meaning and intention.

If Machado de Assis's narrators give us any advice, it is to read attentively. If we are to divine the meaning of Machado de Assis's lapses, subtleties, and teasing, we must understand what he demands of us as readers. He expects us to participate actively in the literary process and not simply to absorb a straightforward story. We must be on our toes, questioning, analyzing, and participating fully as we read the work. A case can be made for this archaically modern technique which combines Sternean appeals to the reader to pay attention and the contemporary idea of reader as collaborator.

PURPOSE OF THE STUDY

The most important element of Machado de Assis's art was his concern with character from the point of view of its exploration and its contrasting in a variety of human situations. The present study, the first in English to apply systematically a philosophical and esthetic critical apparatus to the texts of Machado de Assis, grew out of my interest in the contemporary criticism of narratology as it applies to the theory of character. Narratology may be defined as a method of reading texts according to theoretical and esthetic premises based on the study of such elements as point of view, or the relationships among author, implied author, narrator, characters, and reader; time structures; the structure of irony, satire, and allegory; thematics; and reader-narrator relationship that aid in uncovering the full significance of the texts. Specifically, this method as applied to the texts of Machado de Assis reveals the complexity of narrative structures, Machado de Assis's experimentalism in ancient and modern narrative forms such as satire, allegory, and unreliable narration, and the Brazilian author's extremely modern handling of time in his works. In addition, I include the techniques of "showing," by which the characters reveal themselves through speech, mirrored reflections, silent monologues, evocation by others, dream, and the like, and "telling," by which the narrator narrates or describes, usually employing narrative analysis and including gesture, animal metaphor, metonomy, art metaphors, synecdoche, literary allusion, and so on.

My study is based on a close reading of the texts and of all previous criticism, and maintains a dialogue with this criticism. It analyzes the constituents of characterization such as time and identity, freedom and causality, from the perspectives of narratology and the "raw" techniques that I have referred to above as "showing" and "telling." The results yield a theory of character that tells us a great deal not only about Machado de Assis the artist, but also about his vision of the human condition—and by extension, about the nature of man and himself. It places Machado de Assis within an appropriate context of great world literature.

A reading of the novels of Machado de Assis stimulates a profound response to the questions surrounding human existence. We become involved in the shadowy area of man's relationship to himself and to other human beings. Characters probe such questions as the meaning of an existence limited by time, how to reconcile heart and mind, the resolution of doubt and ambiguity, the inherent conflicts in man's nature which impede fulfillment and the unification of "self." Because the "people" acting out these problems are within the covers of a book, we possess a certain superiority to and the advantage of distance and abstraction from them. If we follow the instructions of the narrative process, we may find a solution to Brás Cubas's dilemma, achieve equilibrium in judging Rubião's conflict, resolve Casmurro's doubt, penetrate the significance of Flora, and share Ayres's epiphany.

On this level of abstraction, we may begin to question how the series of word masses which constitute the characters comes to involve us emotionally and intellectually to such an extent. It does not matter that they are not "real" or even modeled on "real people." Because they reflect aspects of human behavior and values and because the problems they struggle with are found in life, these designs and groupings come to represent absorbing entities whose destinies engage and stimulate us to a degree of intensity often absent in relationships with people we know. In E. M. Forster's view, it is precisely the revelation of the interior life that constitutes the difference between the fictional and the real world. The author knows everything about his characters and may or may not choose to share this knowledge with the reader. A reality impossible to attain in real life comes from this source.[6] Our access to this reality frees us temporarily from all the ambiguity and doubt of our own daily existence because we are allowed to penetrate similar conditions in the lives of the characters and thus achieve an overview of their destiny which we cannot achieve of our own. This ordering of the novelist's universe and its inhabitants which we are allowed to share represents a great artistic achievement. Anybody who has ever tried his hand at drawing character in imaginative literature can testify that it is not a question of a simple manipulation of techniques, but rather one related to the mystery of creation itself, as much an act of imagination on the part of the reader as on that of the writer. While any analytic approach to this mystery can only achieve limited results, it will illuminate the processes which have gone into it and ultimately, reflect a conceptual framework for a theory of character in the novels of a specific author, Machado de Assis.

From his own writing, we know that the most important of novelistic elements for Machado de Assis was character. What interested him above all was man. As early as 1872, he singled out this aspect of his art in the preface to *Resurrection*, in which he desired to explore the contrast between two natures. In his next novel, *The Hand and the Glove* of 1874, he aimed principally at the drawing of the character Guiomar. When asked if he did not care about nature, the Brazilian artist replied that he was only interested in man, man in his interiority, alone and fragile in the face of daily tumults.[7]

Throughout his criticism of Portuguese and Brazilian literature, he commented on the creation of character. In an essay on Joaquim Manuel de Macedo's plays, Machado de Assis insisted that the writer must interest the human heart rather than stimulate curiosity.[8] He praised José de Alencar's creation of Iracema, copied from nature, idealized by art, and displaying a unique soul capable of loving and feeling.[9] Machado de Assis's rather sharp criticism of the character Luisa in *O Primo Basílio* stated that she was a puppet devoid of passions or moral conviction of any kind.[10] The preceding statements reflect Machado de Assis's more positive attitude toward the tradition of romance as opposed to his aversion to the school of naturalism. His participation in this polemic was to constitute an important feature of his literary autonomy.

Given Machado de Assis's concern for and interest in character, a study aimed at establishing a theory of this element in his novels is particularly inviting. While critics such as Ducrot and Todorov can affirm that the category of character has paradoxically remained one of the most obscure of poetics because of the modern reaction to a total submission to it at the end of the nineteenth century,[11] there have been several book-length studies devoted exclusively to this topic since 1960.[12] Previous to these works, many writers and critics have dedicated full or partial discussions to character despite Aristotle's subordination of it to action.[13] The number of recent articles on the subject challenges the impact of Vladimir Propp's reduction of character to a function of plot in folktales, Robbe-Grillet's "elimination" of character from his novels, and Borges's conviction of the value of sustaining interest in plot rather than in character.[14] Whatever course this polemic may take, I believe that the novels of Machado de Assis, like other great literature, exist to explore character.

Of the critical bibliography, many works have been useful to my discussion but the most suggestive in establishing a partial framework for Machado de Assis's theory of character is W. J. Harvey's *Character and the Novel.* Harvey is concerned with the theory of mimesis and considers himself a mimetic critic whose assumptions are based on the proposition that "Art imitates Nature." Departing from his definitions of words like truth, probability, and realism, he attempts to discern their relation to the concept of character. For the mimetic critic, there is no difference between the response to art and to life. He states: "Critical judgments demand the same qualities of intelligence, sensibility, rational control and emotional response that we deploy in our actual lives, though no doubt at a greater pitch and with more concentration and purity than in life itself." Harvey does not believe that what he calls the "texture of life"—manners, social structures, values—provides a stable frame of reference. He finds this in what he calls the "constitutive categories" of time, identity, causality, and freedom. He believes that they are inherent in all experience, that they have important and immediate esthetic concomitants; identities, motive, cause and effect are sufficiently distinct to provide a standard beyond the work of art, a frame of reference located in life itself. A judgment may be made on the basis of these categories of the adequacy of a work's imitation of reality. Truthful handling of them will convince the reader of the "true to lifeness" of the experience portrayed. Because of their slow rate of change, the categories provide a stability adequate for practical purposes. Harvey bases his thesis on an attempt at a mimetic theory within this structure of experience.

How does Harvey's theory apply to the works of Machado de Assis? We know that Machado de Assis's aim was to achieve a reality based on esthetic truth. This had nothing to do with the servile and photographic realism of the school of Zola. In this respect, Harvey's views are quite similar to Machado de Assis's in that the critic's application of the constitutive categories to naturalist art such as *O Crime do Padre Amaro* and *O Primo Basílio* indicates mimetic inadequacy in the limitations placed on freedom and causality. Machado de Assis would have stressed the failure to represent the category of identity as well, witness his criticism of Eça de Queiroz's morally defective puppets. Underlying the consistent occurrence of literary values in Machado de Assis's novels—self-consciousness about literature, parody, self-parody, and the exaggerated role of the narrator who reminds us that the work we are reading is art and not life—the impression of reality is not disturbed. We believe that the traditional classification of Machado de Assis as a realist writer has some basis in fact, but it is only one of the multifarious elements of his art. In my attempt to arrive at a theory of character in Machado de Assis's novels, I hope to reconcile some of these elements.

Like Harvey, I believe that in order to achieve my objective, I must analyze the constituents of character. I diverge somewhat from him in what I consider to be the processes of character. While these are closely interwoven and in some cases, hardly distinguishable, they can be isolated. The first of these is theme. I will attempt to illustrate its relationship to character drawing in pointing out its function as a technique of characterization. Furthermore, if in a theory of character, we must take into consideration the characters' expression and embodiment of values, we may view themes as the basis for an organization of the values underlying actions.

The links between point of view and character have long been observed in literary criticism. In fact, it is the function of the narrator to draw himself and other "people" in the novel. My discussion of this element will focus on its overlapping with characterization as well as on the intricacies of the narrative process itself in which the norms of the work may be divided by a tremendous ironic gap from the narrator, characters, and even from the reader. We will find the participation of the latter in character drawing to be crucial in the works of Machado de Assis. There is an almost chemical reaction which takes place in the creation of "people" within the narrator-reader aspect of the narrative process.

I include time as one of the constituents of character. In this choice, I coincide with one of Harvey's constitutive categories. For him, it is part of the structure of experience itself. Its adequate representation in a work of art contributes to truth. I will also show it as a frame for the telling of a story and as a theme in Machado de Assis's novels. We will see that a psychological reconstruction within time is a constant feature of Machado de Assis's art and a *sine qua non* of character drawing.

In addition to the processes I have mentioned are the "raw" techniques of characterization themselves. These are stimuli to the act of imagination by which the reader and writer create the "people" of the work. I will show that what Machado de Assis does with the words and symbols he uses in his creation reflects his literary autonomy, his reactions to the world around him with its philosophical and literary systems, his ever-present awareness of great literature (particularly Shakespeare), and his dexterity in engaging impressionistic techniques to convey the greatest of moral and spiritual values. On the basis of an analysis of these processes, I hope to show that Machado de Assis's theory of character is rooted in esthetic truth, but is essentially metaliterary, based on the values of great literature and expressed by means of the writer's individuality.

NOTES

1. *Dicionário de Literatura*, 2nd ed., directed by Jacinto do Prado Coelho (Porto: Livraria Figueirinhas, 1971), pp. 965-966.

2. Antonio Cândido, "Esquema de Machado de Assis," in *Vários Escritos* (São Paulo: Livraria Duas Cidades, 1970), p. 24.

3. Joaquim Maria Machado de Assis, "J. M. de Macedo: O Culto do Dever," *Critíca*, in *Machado de Assis Obra Completa*, organized by

Afrânio Coutinho, Vol. III (Rio de Janeiro: Editora José Aguilar Ltda., 1962), p. 847. Hereafter, references to the works of Machado de Assis will be from his collected works, *Machado de Assis Obra Completa*, organized by Afrânio Coutinho, 3 vols. (Rio de Janeiro: Editora José Aguilar Ltda., 1962).

4. Machado de Assis, "O Passado, O Presente e O Futuro da Literatura," *Crítica*, Vol. III, p. 798.

5. Tristão de Ataide, "Machado de Assis, O Critico," in *Machado de Assis Obra Completa*, organized by Afrânio Coutinho, Vol. III (Rio de Janeiro: Editora José Aguilar Ltda., 1962), p. 780.

6. E. M. Forster, *Aspects of the Novel* (New York: Harcourt, Brace and World, Inc., 1954), p. 63.

7. Pontes, op cit., p. 256.

8. Machado de Assis, "O Teatro de Joaquim Manuel de Macedo," *Crítica*, Vol. III, p. 886.

9. Machado de Assis, "Jose de Alencar: Iracema," *Crítica*, Vol. III, p. 850.

10. Machado de Assis, "Eça de Queiroz: O Primo Basílio," *Crítica*, Vol. III, pp. 905, 906, 907.

11. Oswald Ducrot and Tzvetan Todorov, *Dictionnaire Encyclopédique des Sciences du Langage* (Paris: Editions du Seuil, 1972), p. 286.

12. These include John Bayley, *The Characters of Love* (London: Constable, 1960); W. J. Harvey, *Character and the Novel* (London: Chatto and Windus, 1965); William H. Gass, *Fiction and the Figures of Life* (New York: Alfred A. Knopf, 1970); Patrick Swinden, *Unofficial Selves* (London: Macmillan, 1973); and J. Leeds Barroll, *Artificial Persons* (Columbia, S.C.: University of South Carolina Press, 1974).

13. See Bibliography.

14. See "Changing Views of Character," *New Literary History*, Vol. 5, No. 2 (Winter 1974); Martin Price, "The Other Self: Thoughts about Character in the Novel," in *Imagined Worlds*, ed. Maynard Mack and Ian Gregor (London: Methuen and Co., 1968); "People of the Book: Character in Forster's *A Passage to India*," *Critical Inquiry*, Vol. 1, No. 3 (March 1975); Rawdon Wilson, "On Character: A Reply to Martin Price," *Critical Inquiry*, Vol. 2, No. 1 (Autumn 1975); Martin Price, "The Logic of Intensity: More on Character," *Critical Inquiry*, Vol. 2, No. 2 (Winter 1975).

15. Harvey, op. cit., pp. 12, 14, 22, 23.

2

A NOVELIST'S WORKSHOP: THE EARLY WORKS OF MACHADO DE ASSIS

THE period during which Machado de Assis wrote his first four novels, *Resurrection* (1872), *The Hand and the Glove* (1874), *Helena* (1876), and *Iáiá Garcia* (1878), may be considered as his apprenticeship in the art of the novel. Up until this time, he had been involved in journalism and had produced essays, criticism, poetry, translations, short stories, and plays, but it is in these four novels that we encounter many of the features which were to go into the creation of the later masterpieces. Despite concessions to the tradition of romance, the early novels demonstrate facets of what was to constitute Machado de Assis's literary autonomy, such as the exploration of psychological aspects of character and the contrast of character in various situations, time as a theme, the irony or distance that separates the values of the implied author from those of the narrator, and a sometimes comic but demanding relationship between narrator and reader.[1] Machado de Assis was extremely conscious of the craft of the novel and from the outset, it would seem that he wished to include the reader in the creative process. Gérard Genette's evaluation of Borges and Proust seems appropriate to the Brazilian master in this context as well: "Le véritable auteur du récit n'est pas seulement celui qui le raconte, mais aussi, et parfois bien davantage, celui que l'écoute. Et qui n'est pas nécessairement celui à qui l'on s'adresse: il y a toujours du monde à côté."[2] On the basis of these criteria, Machado de Assis emerges as a writer of the present rather than of the late nineteenth century.

RESSURREIÇÃO (RESURRECTION)

From his earliest novel, *Resurrection*, Machado de Assis showed a dominant interest in character and an original treatment of this element. At a moment when Brazilian romanticism was analyzing customs and characteristic types, the author of *Resurrection* could say: "I did not wish to write a novel of customs; I attempted to outline a situation and the contrast of two characters; with these simple elements I sought the interest of the book" (*R*, p. 114). In effect, the relationship between the idealistic Lívia and the doubt-ridden and cynical Félix leads only to frustration and lack of fulfillment for both.

To begin discussion of *Resurrection*, I would like to explore two elements of the novel very closely related to character—thematics and point of view. The themes of *Resurrection* are particularly significant because we find them throughout the novels of Machado de Assis. The most important among them in *Resurrection* is essential to an understanding of the male protagonist, ironically named Félix. Quoting Shakespeare, Machado de Assis announced in the foreword to the first edition of the work: "Our doubts are traitors, and make us lose the good we oft might win by fearing to attempt." Félix's principal trait is doubt and all that this implies. He does not believe in love or rather, believes only in the transiency of human passions. In the opening chapter, we see him breaking off an affair of six months. He explains his behavior by asserting that his loves are all semestral; they last longer than roses, they last for two seasons. For his heart a year is eternity. After six months, love packs its bags and leaves the heart like a traveler leaves a hotel; boredom enters afterward—a bad guest (*R*, pp. 121, 122). An echo to this sentiment is acted out by the character Cecília, Félix's former mistress, who easily accommodates herself to the limited duration of her sentimental attachments. A related theme, and one that points to others in the novel, is time. It is essentially destructive of human emotions and leads inevitably to death. Within its flux, we nourish illusions which only the experience of reality can correct. Death and illusion versus reality are linked to the theme of the novel's title, resurrection. If Félix could overcome his doubt and its outward manifestation, jealousy, he might be resurrected from his living death by means of Lívia's love. For short periods throughout the narrative, love appears to triumph only to be defeated by Félix's doubt. Thus, the resurrection does not take place.

Fear of life and failure is another of the interrelated themes of the novel, symbolically expressed in the metaphor of navigation and shipwreck. One such metaphor is Félix's advice to Meneses comparing the experience of love affairs to storms at sea: "It isn't on land that sailors are made, but on the ocean, confronting the storm" (*R*, p. 130). Félix again comments in nautical figures on the contrast between Lívia's relatively sheltered experience of life and his own—disastrous according to him: "You were shipwrecked in sight of land, he said, and you only got your clothing wet. Do you know what it is to be shipwrecked on the high seas alone and to lose everything, even life? That's how it was for me" (*R*, p. 153). There are further references to life as the sea, people as navigators, and the constant peril of storm, shipwreck, and the possibility of self-sacrifice in acting as life raft for others. The network of *Resurrection's* themes refers predominantly to Félix with contrasts and echoes in other characters and thus serves as a device of characterization. The means of reproducing this network is the actual telling of the story or point of view.

In a sense, the narrator of *Resurrection* is a character in the novel even though he does not participate directly in the events narrated. He foreshadows the narrator-agents of the later works and sets a pattern for them. He readily enters the narrative, revealing his plans, intentions, and progress.[3] He openly refers to himself as "I" and alludes to his program of characterization: "The essence of his character will become better known upon reading these pages and accompanying the hero through the unexpected reversals of this most simple action which I will undertake to narrate" (*R*, p. 116). Here we have an indication of Machado de Assis's process of characterization, which is to sketch the character and then follow him through events in which the original outline is in part filled in by the reader. The narrator constantly explains motives, describes interior states, and makes judgments. During his appearances, he engages in minor philosophical discussions or digressions. When he discusses the merits of different kinds of love, he makes an equivocal judgment on the subject. He leaves it to the Doctors of Scripture to evaluate these loves. He cannot decide. Both are loves, both have their energies (*R*, p. 142). He asks questions for the reader's benefit and answers them directly as when Félix believes that Lívia's intentions toward him as manifested by a hand shake are not what he thought them to be. To his own question of whether Lívia's hand shake could be chance or illusion, he replies that it certainly was an illusion: an illusion or chance but since the doctor did not perceive this immediately, he made his first error in judging the widow (*R*, p. 131). On the other occasions, he addresses the reader and refers to his own omniscience—I who am telling you this story—to clarify actions. In this instance, he tells us that the anonymous letter accusing Lívia of having betrayed her dead husband is from the villain of the piece, Luís Batista. The role of *Resurrection*'s narrator points to his unlimited omniscience at a time when Flaubert and the realist-naturalist schools as well as Henry James were insisting on the "disappearance" of the narrator, a certain playful attitude toward the reader, and to an effort to include the reader in the creative process.

The implied author's creation of the reader takes various forms in the telling of the story. On occasion, the narrator begins a summary of character or events by addressing the reader affectionately —friend reader (*amigo leitor*)—reminiscent of eighteenth-century English narratives. Elsewhere, he scoldingly calls the reader impatient as he explains why certain events do not take place. The demand for reader collaboration is fully developed in the later works but as in the case of other features already discussed, it appears in embryo in the early works. When the narrator asks what appears to be a rhetorical question in the text, he is anticipating the reader's curiosity. His answer is both a means of edification and of characterizing: "Could she understand then what a painful and weighty obligation she had contracted? Maybe not. She confided in herself, in the prestige of her love, in Félix's heart, to conquer all and to realize what was now the dream of her life." (R, p. 143). Within the context of the story, the reader now understands why Lívia persists in the seemingly sterile relationship with Félix and he also sees Lívia acting out the idealism of her initial characterization.

In sharing his omniscience with the reader, the narrator makes the latter aware of the characters' imperfect knowledge of each other. In so doing, he is once again in the process of character drawing as when he analyzes Lívia's perception of Félix. Her love for him prevents her from seeing Félix as he is—skeptical, weak, and inconstant. If she had been listening not only with her heart, she would have perceived more than Félix's grievances and bitterness. She would have seen that Félix was naturally weak-hearted in addition to the disillusionments he had experienced (R, p. 154). The idea of the privilege of narrator and reader in the ability to understand completely the fictional characters even when they themselves do not occurs more explicitly in *The Hand and the Glove*. According to E. M. Forster, this is why fictional characters seem more real than characters in history or even our own friends; we know everything about them.[4] In the world of the characters, however, the ambiguity of life is reproduced. While the narrator and reader know what Raquel's smile indicates in the following passage—she thinks that Meneses and Lívia are in love—Lívia interpets and reacts to the error of this perception: "What did that benevolent but sly smile fluttering on her lips mean? Meneses who was looking outdoors didn't see it, but the widow saw it and was startled" (R, p. 159). At another point, the implied author concedes insight to his character and appears to agree with his evaluation of another. Leafing through an old poetry album, the protagonist comes upon a poem whose mediocrity of form is surpassed only by that of its thought. The narrator ridicules the lame and infirm of Parnassus, thus setting forth his value which coincides with Félix's. In their opinion, the poet, Lívia's dead husband, was a fool.

In spite of being an effective means of character drawing, this coincidence of values between the narrator and Félix is unusual in the novel. In general, there is quite a distance between these two entities. This appears quite distinctly in the initial characterization. Félix has not distinguished himself in any way by the age of thirty-six and has been saved from mediocrity by an unexpected inheritance, an admittedly theatrical device in the novel (*R*, p. 115). Félix's history indicates that he is weak and barring a radical change in his character, he will remain an idle, unambitious, and futile personage in the novel. We accept the narrator's evaluation of Félix and observe the enactment of his negative traits at the same time that we observe and accept the positive version of this process in Lívia. No irony seems to be intended. The narrator's values are clearly spelled out. Similarly, there seems to be no distance between the values of the implied author and the narrator. In fact, the narrator's straightforward declarations convey the norms of the book and of the implied author. Love is the supreme human value and in a harmonious marriage, fiery passions are substituted by reciprocity of confidence and mutual esteem (*R*, p. 123). The contrast to these values is expressed in the drawing of the negative or villainous personages such as Félix and Luís Batista. Thus the implied author-narrator relationship is not marked in this work by the distance of similar relationships in the later works.

All of the elements pertinent to the telling of a story are partially structured by time. The narration occurs ten years after the actual events: "On that day—ten years ago!" (*R*, p. 115). Events are narrated chronologically over a period of approximately one year. The action starts on New Year's Day and references to sequences of half hours, hours, that evening, a little while later, the next day, two weeks later, a few days later, two days later, and so on, provide the time structure for the recounting of the novel. In the early chapters, the segments are devoted to the introduction of characters, their relating to the protagonists, and the interaction of Lívia and Félix. As the novel progresses, sentimental crises of increasing intensity take place within specific time references. These are followed by other segments in which discussions and commentary on what the parties involved in the crises are feeling. Thus, at the very beginning of the novel, Félix breaks off a relationship with Cecília. One half hour later, he leaves her house and meets Meneses, with whom he discusses the affair. That evening Félix sees Lívia at a party, and all the time sequences following are preparatory for the seven or eight crises that occur during the year of their relationship. The preparatory sequences mainly show the contrast of these two personages, a device of characterization. Sleep and the passage from night to day are mentioned when the characters are perturbed or calm about their emotional lives. When a seemingly neutral encounter takes place within a specific time reference, such as Viana's discussion with Félix about his birthday dinner, it is a prelude to yet another sentimental crisis. At the dinner, Luís, Lívia's son, asks Félix why he doesn't marry his mother and consequently sets off a chain reaction among Raquel, Lívia, Félix, and Meneses. It is clear that although the references to time are chronometric, to the characters time is subjective or emotional. After Félix breaks off for the second time, his remorse is so great that the night seems longer than the day, which had seemed very long indeed. While waiting to be married, the days seem long to the lovers, short to Meneses and Raquel who, ignorant of the protagonists' engagement, are enamored of Lívia and Félix respectively. The subject matter of *Resurrection's* time structure is highly emotional and novelistic in the sense that it does not reflect a routine of daily life like that outside fiction but the most dramatic moments within fiction.

The characters do not all share in the implied author's conception of time. For Félix, it is chronometric and seems to measure the duration of his passions. For his heart, a year is eternity. Like Brás Cubas, he is convinced of the transiency of human passions. As in other matters, Lívia and Félix are not in agreement on this point. For her, emotional time has nothing to do with the clock and everything to do with the value of the experience. These two conceptions of time further contrast the protagonists. While Lívia the idealist gives full rein to the interplay of imagination and experience and consequently achieves a kind of freedom from time, Félix is a prisoner of irreversible chronometric time.

As we have seen, both thematics and point of view are not only intimately tied to characterization but specifically function as agents of this process in *Resurrection*. While recognizing that the boundaries of these elements are tenuous, I believe that an attempt to isolate further Machado de Assis's craftsmanship in this area will assist in understanding his conception of character.

For the most part, Machado de Assis's techniques of characterization in *Resurrection* are commonly found in the nineteenth-century novel, but if we compare them with those of Eça de Queiroz in his naturalist phase, we are struck by the absence in Machado de Assis's novels of the multiple angle view of character, the accumulation of descriptive details, and of free indirect style. This is not surprising if we consider Machado de Assis's aversion to the school of Zola which he referred to as *realismo*.[5] Machado de Assis's method is progressive, as observed previously. The initial sketch is filled in as the story is narrated. In general, there is more summary (telling) than scene (showing). In his book, *The Craft of Fiction* (1968), Percy Lubbock systematizes Henry James's theories on the advantages of "showing" over "telling" or the "disappearance" of the narrator. Wayne Booth (*The Rhetoric of Fiction*, 1961) points out that certain novels are just as effective in "telling" as others are in "showing." Thus, Félix is successfully drawn by means of extensive summary including narrative analysis. It is the narrator who explains the substance of Félix's elegant dilettantism. Although trained as a medical doctor, his inheritance permits him to live a life of ease filled with stylish pastimes. By means of description, the narrator conveys Félix's physical appearance. His looks are average but distinguished by refined taste in clothing. His expression reflects his moral being, that of a man who distrusts feelings and for the most part, has turned them off. Another technique of characterization is silent monologue. Utilizing the nautical motif again, a motif which represents danger for Félix, the protagonist expresses his doubts about the sincerity of Lívia's feelings for him. He cynically imagines that she is simply setting the stage for a transient affair which is all he is capable of contemplating. He assumes that she feels as he does and is justifying her surrender through her passionate declarations. He believes that it would have been better if they had navigated close to the shore (*R*, p. 139).

Self-revelation through dialogue with other characters (showing), demonstrates Félix's mistaken ideas about love and emphasizes his mistrust of feelings. He thinks emotional matters can be resolved through the intellect and by suppressing the heart. When Meneses asks where he can find this resolve, Félix indicates his head.

Meneses responds that the head has nothing to do with this; all the damage is in the heart. Félix advises him to cut out the disease by the root by suppressing his heart (*R*, p. 132). The occurrence of gesture is sparse but in one instance where it is used, it mirrors one of Félix's basic traits, his cynicism, as Viana sings Lívia's praises: "A slight smile curled Félix's lip, while Viana went on with the panegyric of his sister with an enthusiasm which could have been sincere and interested at the same time" (*R*, p. 119).

Animal metaphor occurs once in the drawing of Félix. He becomes a "wild and indomitable bronco" when he discovers that the bonds of love have tied him (*R*, p. 142). Characterization through contrast is yet another device utilized in defining the roles of the principal characters as we have seen. It functions similarly in secondary relationships. Meneses is Félix's foil in every way. He is sincere, open, and disposed to loving—qualities that place Félix's doubting cynicism in relief. Meneses is an echo of Lívia and at one point, Félix tells him that he is like her.

José Aderaldo Castello observes that in Machado de Assis's characterizations, descriptive elements are sparse and reduced to references which the reader must fill in.[6] This view coincides with the program outlined above particularly in its distinction from naturalist techniques. More important is the reference to the reader's collaboration. We have seen that it is this element in combination with the narrator's role that is the key to character drawing in *Resurrection*. This feature is encountered throughout Machado de Assis's novels.

The techniques of Lívia's portraiture differ from Félix's in that she is often evoked by other people in the novel. Her physical aspect is conveyed through Félix's eyes. He sees a very beautiful woman whose manners enhance the total effect of her appeal. She is further endowed with a smooth brunette complexion, classical features, and a reflective expression (*R*, p. 128). Raquel points out her rival's regal bearing by referring to her as a queen. Viana, her brother, comments on Lívia's moral makeup—in his opinion, her idealism is romantic. The narrator later underscores this evaluation in summary. Lívia often leaves the practical realm to ascend the heights of an ideal world.

Among the secondary characters, certain techniques of elaboration that appear in the later works are present. On occasion, bird and animal imagery occurs to point out features of various characters. Thus, the contrast of falcons and doves and of lions and does indicates human characteristics of aggressiveness and docility. Lívia's son, Luís, is a *ficelle* in that his presence assists in the telling of the story. It is his existence that changes the tone of Félix's intentions toward Lívia and his comment that brings to a climax the triangle Lívia-Raquel-Félix. Raquel is portrayed by means of an art metaphor. She is one of those porcelain vases that one is afraid of breaking.

Through the techniques of character drawing the novel's personages are established, but their souls or "life-likeness" are brought about in another way. Castello asserts that once the scheme of the characters' confrontation in which they seek a common destiny is completed, the narrator concludes a narrative in which the moral takes precedence over the psychological. The individual is responsible for his acts. It is he who constructs his illusion or myth or makes them impossible through lost faith although the narrator suggests the obscure force of destiny.[7] While Machado de Assis's ideal in relation to character drawing was to unite human passions with the original touches of poetry, a thought expressed in his criticism[8] and one which points to a desire to keep his characters in touch with their feelings, I take exception to the declaration that the moral takes precedence over the psychological in this novel. In my view, the implications of the precedence of the moral over the psychological would be related to a conflict between good and evil and a conscious choice to be made or; having been made therein. Félix is unhappy because he does not follow his heart but all his actions are calculated by his mental being. His springs of action are essentially psychological and they are what determine the outcome of his confrontation with a character who comes closer to Machado de Assis's moral ideal. As for the narrator's suggestions of the obscure force of destiny, Machado de Assis was to spell out clearly his conception of causality in literature in his final novel, *Counselor Ayres' Memorial*.[9] Like life, literature blends the casual and the causal, things are connected and contingent, patterned and random, we are both free and determined.[10] In this sense, if circumstances had favored the realization of marriage between Lívia and Félix, the latter's psychological makeup would never have permitted the couple to be happy. Thus, when Castello affirms that the narrator reveals the fates of all the characters ten years after the events of the narrative in a sententious manner, I believe that the critic has missed the mark. It is not destiny that made Félix unhappy but his psychic imprisonment or the fact that he did not exercise his freedom over the psychological forces that dominated him. Lívia, on the other hand, remained free to pursue her dream and while we find her withdrawal from society by the age of thirty-four somewhat incongruous, that is a matter of relative chronological values.

Resurrection indicates a basic pattern for Machado de Assis's later characters. In contrast to the ideals of his implied author, the realization of love and human beings capable of feeling and acting in accordance with this end, the Brazilian master shows a series of psychological aberrations from these norms. Félix is the first in a long succession of such characters.

A MÃO E A LUVA (THE HAND AND THE GLOVE)

The Hand and the Glove appeared in 1874. It is thought to represent continued progress in Machado de Assis's technique as well as a regression to existing patterns of Victorianism, the predominance of environmental influence, the effort to wipe out psychological penetration, and the substitution of the play of romantic situations which unfold into the social picture of the second reign in Brazil. *Resurrection*, in contrast, was a departure from the beaten path which would lead eventually to Machado de Assis's masterpieces.[11] Despite Barreto Filho's declaration, many of the elements of the later novels occur in the three immediately following *Resurrection*. The experimental aspect of these novels, in my opinion, has not received its due attention. As in his first novel, Machado de Assis was again concerned with character in his second. In its foreword, he stated, "I ought to say that the drawing of such characters—that of Guiomar, especially—was my principal objective, if not my exclusive one, the action serving only as a canvas upon which I cast the contour of the profiles. Although they are incomplete, I wonder if they might have come out natural and true" (*HG*, p. 3).

As in *Resurrection*, themes are closely identified with character and serve as characterizing agents. The effectiveness of will is to Luís Alves what doubt is to Félix, but instead of failure, it represents success. It is the vehicle for his professional and personal fulfillment, political triumph, and the winning of Guiomar. The marriage of convenience refers to Jorge, nephew to the Baroness, Guiomar's protectress. The theme of the excesses of the tradition of romance is carried forward by Estevão, Guiomar's third suitor, while that of upward mobility resides in the heroine's own experience as the child of modest parents who die when she is young. She has a short career as a teacher and is ultimately adopted by a baroness. Illusion versus reality again makes an appearance, as in Machado de Assis's other novels but in this case, the two are made to coincide because of the dominance of will on the part of Luís Alves and Guiomar. Paralleling *Resurrection*, there are images of the sea, storms, tides, and navigation in the second novel. Estevão's romantic love for Guiomar is compared to a storm at sea which had subsided leaving only the strong pull of the tide (*ressaca*), an image familiar to readers of *Dom Casmurro*. Guiomar's imagination, relevant to the theme of illusion and reality, is compared to a sailing vessel in which we all embark when life on land becomes tiresome in order to navigate on the high seas. Also present in *The Hand and the Glove* is the equine imagery of Machado de Assis's first novel. Guiomar's heart was born with reins on; while it trots, canters, or gallops, it never runs away nor does it lose itself or its horse (*HG*, p. 65). The image relates to the balance between feeling and will in the female protagonist. As Estevão's imagination gives way to romantic fantasies, Luís Alves deems it best not to interrupt it in its course, a judgment expressed in equine imagery: "Luís Alves decided it would be wise not to frighten the horses. His imagination raced, raced, raced along, reins free, and there was a smile on his lips" (*HG*, p. 9).

In the telling of the story, the relationship between narrator and reader is even more developed than in *Resurrection* and serves to produce a comic effect. The narrator makes it clear that he will share his omniscience with the reader and answers the questions he anticipates from the latter. He specifically states: ". . . but it is the privilege of the writer and the reader to see in the face of a character that which others do not or cannot see" (*HG*, pp. 75, 76). The narrator of *The Hand and the Glove* is very conscious of his role and privilege. After describing Guiomar in great detail, he comments that Estevão, who was observing her from a distance, could not see all this, but he, as the teller of stories, is duty bound to report all (*HG*, p. 18). At another point, he refers to Estevão's fantasy about Guiomar dissociating himself from its content. He declares that it is not he speaking; he simply and faithfully writes down the lover's thoughts (*HG*, p. 97). In addition to completing the reader's knowledge of the characters, the narrator digresses on the subjects of love and life. He speculates as to whether Guiomar's thoughts about her disappointed suitor, Estevão, are philosophical as she gazes at the eternal and apathetic sky. He concludes that she is too full of life to be preoccupied with the past. Her thoughts are on the present and the future.

If the narrator shares with the reader, he also teases him about his curiosity to know what will happen next. He tells the reader to wait a while, to have patience, and lets him know when he will satisfy his curiosity. Throughout the narrative, he refers to the reader as "my lady reader," "the reader," and as "perspicacious reader," indicating that sometimes the implied author's reader is also an ideal reader..He assumes that the reader is fully involved in the story, knows the characters, has opinions about events and personages, and has already reached certain conclusions before being told about them. The narrator's confidential relationship with the reader includes revealing his artistic intentions to the latter: "It is probably not necessary to tell the reader who is discerning and benevolent—(oh! especially benevolent, because one must have good will and a great deal of it in order to have come this far and to be able to continue to the end of a story like this, in which the author is more concerned with painting one or two characters and exposing a few human feelings than he is with doing anything else, because anything else he could not manage to do) . . ." (*HG*, p. 50).

The narrator's role in this novel is a preview of his Sternean counterpart in *Epitaph of a Small Winner*.[12] As in the latter novel, there exists a degree of distance or irony, although much more limited, between the values of the implied author and those of the narrator as well as the more generalized irony in regard to art. While the narrator of *The Hand and the Glove* pokes fun at the product of the European tradition of romance—Estevão has been formed by the reading of Goethe and Byron—and ridicules poets like Estevão who observe all the rules of versifying and consult a dictionary of rhymes, it is clear that there is sympathy for this character. Guiomar recognizes the value of his affection and the implied author's judgment of the efficacy of will juxtaposed to Estevão's misery is not without irony. Machado de Assis's sympathy for the sentimental in this novel may be a metaphor for his attitude toward the tradition of romance, one of affection.[13] Echoing the action of *The Hand and the Glove*, Machado de Assis's striking out on an autonomous route may indicate his exertion of will in the esthetic realm despite his predilection for the school of Goethe.

In *The Hand and the Glove*, there seems to be a better balance between showing and telling than in the first novel. Recalling Barreto Filho's observation cited above, what we are shown is a portrait of the second reign in Brazil. More time and care have apparently gone into the scenes of the *chácara* (county estate), its morning episode in the garden, and in the evoking of the social life of a certain class which takes place among small conversational groups standing or sitting in the living rooms of great houses. Historical street names lend concreteness to the picture, which unfolds before us, of a period twenty years anterior to the telling of the events. Guiomar's story unfolds in 1853.

Time is more complex in this novel than in its predecessor. It flows chronologically in references to the hour of day or night, a little while later, noon the next day, one month later, two years later, two weeks later, and so on, and as in life outside fiction, it is marked by notable events in Rio de Janeiro's cultural history, such as the battle of rival fans of different opera singers. Certain episodes are told in flashback, as is Guiomar's story which reveals the psychological and moral elements of her formation. The narrator makes references to information given in past chapters, a characteristic feature of the later works. The subject matter treated within the specific time sequences is the portrayal of the characters, their emotional crises, and discussion of or commentary on both. Thus, in the opening scene, Estevão is in the midst of a crisis of unrequited love. During his confession to Luís Alves, both he and Luís are characterized and Guiomar makes her first appearance in the novel through flashback. Estevão is never mentioned without reference to his sentimental life, a means of drawing this Brazilian Werther. Guiomar's appearances are always accompanied by the evocation of her physical, intellectual, moral, and esthetic attributes. She is the center of all the discussion of sentimental crises. The talk about matters of the heart occupies the greatest number of time sequences; second most frequent on the scale is characterization; least frequent are the crises themselves. This scheme reflects Machado de Assis's intentions, cited above, in which action is secondary to character drawing. The greater part of the narrator's attention is devoted to depicting the characters whose time, in turn, is devoted more to the discussion of sentimental crises than to participation in them. The narrator and the reader are aware of the passage of objective time, but time experienced by the characters is subjective, witness Estevão's unlimited suffering and Luís Alves's calculated manipulation of clock time to gain a goal which can only be his within the rhythm of Guiomar's "time."

Like its treatment in *Resurrection*, time in the second novel is nominally divided into chronometric and subjective realms. The two have nothing to do with each other: ". . . and thus the hours of the night drained along, while the clock in the dining room registered them dryly and systematically, as if reminding our two dear friends that man's passions neither accelerate nor moderate the rhythm of time" (*HG*, p. 10). The wrong-headed character, Mrs. Oswald, associates the heart with mechanical time while the more informed narrator, mocking and always conscious of literary effects, knows better: "But to that youthful and impatient heart, each minute seemed, well, I won't say a century—that would be to abuse my rights of style—but an hour; it certainly seemed to him like an hour" (*HG*, p. 19). In short, it is emotional and not chronometric time that determines the values of one's life. Thus, the time in which life is most fulfilling on this level is considered an individual's "time." His "time" is always better than that of others.

As in the preceding category, the creation of character in *The Hand and the Glove* shows progress over the same technique in *Resurrection*. Guiomar is first briefly sketched in terms of age and occupation. She is a seventeen-year-old student teacher. By means of metonymy, she reappears two years later as a dressing gown (*um roupão*) walking in the Baroness's garden. Art metaphors describe her exquisite taste in clothing, the frame of a beautiful panel. The narrator analyzes her appeal, which spoke more to the intellect than to the senses, and employs a metaphor of the beautiful butterfly that emerged from a cocoon in the flashback to her origins. Narrative analysis is employed to explain her motives—she needs the brilliant life—while the Baroness and Mrs. Oswald evoke other characteristics in dialogue during which they contemplate the young lady's marriage to Jorge, the Baroness's mediocre nephew. Mrs. Oswald allays the Baroness's fears that Guiomar might love someone other than her nephew in observing Guiomar's idiosyncrasies. She points out the young woman's inconstancy and expresses her doubt that Guiomar will ever have a great passion. In view of the calculating that goes into the match Guiomar finally makes, Mrs. Oswald's judgment about her was quite correct but the Englishwoman's prediction of the young woman's malleability was mistaken.

The effectiveness of the character drawing of the three men who aspire to Guiomar's hand is established through contrast. Luís is the realist, Estevão, the sentimental dreamer, and Jorge, the superficial and upper-class dandy. Each man is characterized by his speech. Luís's is direct—an advantage when his tête-à-tête with Guiomar is about to be interrupted by Jorge. His declaration gains in sincerity from its simplicity and its content is calculated to appeal to Guiomar's psychology. His first step is to ask nothing but to show interest and approval.

Estevão's speech is florid. He speaks habitually in hyperboles of passion made of blood and a life of suffering until death. Far from being in control of his destiny, an attribute the ambitious Guiomar could respect, Estevão believes himself to be under the influence of an evil star. In romantic imagery, he asserts that this love is the blood of his blood and the life of his life. He cannot forget Guiomar. It would be well if he could, but his ill-fated destiny tears even that hope from him. He believes that this incessant inner misery will follow him to his death (*HG*, p. 96).

Jorge's speech is affected. It reflects his lack of conviction and sincerity and is colored by bad metaphors and maddening circumlocutions. Luís interrupts him so that he will get to the point.

While the summary of Luís Alves's character is not particularly sympathetic—he is ambitious, cold, and resolute as well as possessor of great presence of mind—he is the most suited to Guiomar's aspirations and he understands her.

Estevão may be a condor, capable of looking toward the sun, but without wings to fly to it. He throws aside his law books to daydream in the garden, compares Guiomar to a Shakespearean fairy or a Klopstockian angel, writes "Byronic" poetry, and identifies with Werther. He indulges in silent monologues in which he contemplates suicide: "I have no other way out, he thought. I must die. There is only one pain and then there is freedom" (*HG*, p. 68). In sum, he is an ineffective masochist. Hurting himself is a need and a pleasure. The narrator indicates that Estevão's soul felt a singular need, the satisfaction of turning the blade in the wound—the voluptuousness of pain (*HG*, p. 115).

Jorge's characterization through summary reveals his age and moral traits. He is proud of his birth, has no occupation, lives from his inheritance, and is measured and superficial in his affections. He would not consider marriage to Guiomar if it were thought to be a misalliance nor does he perceive her according to her true value. Sensuality is the main focus of his view of Guiomar, whom he compares to Venus.

Throughout, the narrator comments on his function of characterizing: "It is wise to say, in order to give the picture a final stroke of the brush . . ." (*HG*, p. 80). This feature of Machado de Assis's art was also observed in the analysis of *Resurrection*.

Machado de Assis's conception of character in *The Hand and the Glove* lacks, as expressed in Barreto Filho's view, psychological penetration. While the characters appear more typical than those of *Resurrection*, Estevão emerges as a metaphor for Machado de Assis's view of the tradition of romance while the protagonists' fulfillment of love based on conscientiously directed will rather than spontaneity would seem to introduce a degree of irony into his character drawing. Technical innovations and the Sterne-like narrator all foreshadow the greater works to come.

HELENA

Machado de Assis's third novel, *Helena*, is striking in its distinctiveness from the first two. Published in 1876, its exaggerated utilization of the conventions of romance has created the impression that it might be a parody of those conventions.[14] Machado de Assis's own apology in the foreword to a reedition of the novel would appear to refute this conclusion. He stated, "Don't criticize me for what you may find romantic. Of the novels I wrote then, I prized this one particularly. Even now that I have gone on to other different pages, I hear a remote echo upon reading these, an echo of youth and ingenuous faith. It is clear that under no circumstances could their past form be changed; each work is appropriate to its time."[15] One critic has suggested that the novel may have been written some years before its publication and therefore could have preceded *Resurrection* and *The Hand and the Glove.*[16] For Helen Caldwell, *Helena* represents an advance in Machado de Assis's early declared esthetic goal of presenting the drama resulting from the emotional conflicts of the characters.[17] In this sense, we may view the novel as another area of Machado de Assis's development and preparation for the later works. Although *Helena* lacks in pure technique in comparison with the first two novels, its characters are more complex. Once again, certain themes may be identified with personages in the novel. The concatenation of these themes is equal to plot which, in turn, reflects the complexity of character.

The theme of upward mobility is associated with Helena while that of incest hovers over Estácio and Camargo. Pride as a theme refers to Helena, the marriage of convenience is of Camargo's domain as is that of self-love, and the theme of obedience to society's conventions falls on Helena and Estácio. The unifying theme is the biblical idea of the sins of the fathers being visited upon their offspring. It is the defunct Counselor Valle's testamentary recognition of Helena as his illegitimate daughter that brings all the characters and their emotions into play.

The narrator of *Helena* is much less obvious than those of its predecessors. Although he refers to himself as "I," is omniscient, enters the characters' consciousnesses at will, and engages frequently in narrative analysis of motives, he withholds complete knowledge from the reader in order to preserve mystery. Unlike the narrators of Henry James and Flaubert, the story teller of *Helena* follows the standards of the traditional novel in that he digresses and offers opinions about events. His comments, however, are limited and unexuberant in comparison with those of Machado de Assis's previous novels. In like manner, the narrator's relationship to the reader is limited and indirect.

The main interaction is among personages who are largely in ignorance of each other. Although the narrator partially reveals the characters, he sustains suspense by not answering their questions, which presumably anticipate those of the reader. Thus, the filling in of the initial sketch is more of a challenge in the reading of *Helena*.

The perceptions of the individuals themselves are not clear in relation to events. In thinking about Helena, Estácio does not realize that he is in love with his sister nor does he guess that she is not his sister and that the object of her passion is Estácio. Helena's origins are further clouded by a dialogue with Camargo, her visits to the house of the blue flag, and the appearance of a mysterious letter. Even after clarification by means of another letter, doubt persists. Other characters are responsible for revealing the principal characters' motives. Father Melchior tells Estácio of the latter's incestuous love for Helena and later advises him of the impossibility of marriage to the young woman even when they themselves know that she is no relation. Society thinks of her as such and thus determines their comportment.

The implied author's values do not reflect distance between those of the narrator and protagonists. Like Estácio, he believes in personal happiness over public power and prestige. Like Helena, he values pride and moral integrity. He and the reader can overlook the falseness of her position since she has been victimized and made into a pawn by people she loves and respects. Camargo is the self-seeking villain whose truly incestuous love for his daughter is a reflection of self-love. His daughter, Eugenia, is frivolous and functions as a foil to Helena.

The time of the narrative's events is dated from Counselor Valle's death—eight o'clock on the night of April 25, 1859. As in the first two novels, time is measured out in chronometric sequences—the next day, ten o'clock the next morning, a little later, weeks later, one Monday, the first days of August, and so on, through a period of approximately one year. While the early segments are partially devoted to character drawing, the dominant tone of the events narrated is one of melodrama. The air is thick with it from the first scene in which Camargo hints that Counselor Valle's final act might have been an error. The reading of Valle's will reveals the crisis, the recognition of an illegitimate daughter who is to be brought up in the midst of the family. All of the subsequent action revolves around the question of Helena's identity from the perspectives of the other characters both in terms of her origins and the enigma she poses. Thus, many time segments are devoted to dialogues about Helena among her fellow characters. Some time passes without much happening, as when Helena spends the greater part of three days in her room upon her arrival at the Valle household. Although no remarkable events take place during certain periods, the narrator elaborates Helena's interaction with the Valle family and their society, a means of characterization. Similarly, episodes during which Estácio interacts with Eugenia are a contrast to his relations with Helena, shown through dialogue and progressing from his sense of Helena's enigma and mystery to suspicion, jealousy, and the melodrama of their mutual recognition of love at the side of her deathbed. The sensational and romantic element occupies other time sequences, such as Camargo's interview with Helena in which he blackmails her, and Salvador's evocation of Helena's history. Thus, the manipulation of time leads up to the sensational events in the novel, but it shows some lapses, perhaps a result of the author's inexperience, a factor which might corroborate the hypothesis that Helena was written before *Resurrection* and *The Hand and the Glove*.

References to the past occur in the mentioning of Estácio's mother's death when he was eighteen, and Helena's mother's death when she was twelve. In Salvador's narrative, a flashback explaining his paternal relationship to Helena and his abandonment by her mother who became Valle's mistress, there seems to be a temporal discrepancy. Helena was twelve when she renewed contact with her real father, Salvador. A year hence her mother was dead, making her thirteen at the time of that event. Another discrepancy occurs in the Aguilar Edition of *Machado de Assis's Complete Works* when Helena presents Estácio with a drawing dated June 25, 1850. In reality, she had done the drawing within the durative time of the narrative in 1859.

Time in *Helena* has the germ of philosophical and emotional as well as chronometric aspects. Helena's eyes are the clock which measures a fateful hour while the clock of affliction and hope measures out extraordinarily long hours. In dialogue with Estácio, Helena points out the value of subjective over mechanical time. She asserts that the main thing is not to do a great deal in a short time, it is to do a great deal that is gratifying or useful. She points out that for a slave, the most gratifying thing is perhaps walking in freedom which will lengthen his journey and will make him forget his enslavement. It is an hour of pure liberty (*H*, pp. 294-295).

It is no wonder that Estácio finds Helena somewhat of an enigma considering her philosophical ratiocinations on such profound topics as freedom and time. She is, after all, a nineteenth-century Brazilian girl of seventeen whose education was probably limited to the three R's, a little French, and piano lessons. The attribute is a feature of Helena's idealization.

If we turn now to Machado de Assis's techniques of character drawing, we observe a phenomenon that heightens mystery. Helena is a figure out of the tradition of romance. Her angelic portrait is idealized, but while the implied author is creating this picture, he is setting the scene for the unfolding of plot. The reader is immediately struck by the contrast of Helena's angelic figure with the defect her brother notices, her expression of sly curiosity and suspicious reserve. On the basis of this, Machado de Assis's character drawing would seem to combine aspects of the tradition of the novel with those of romance. He emphasizes her complexion, peach brunette. He points out that the pure and severe lines of her face appeared to have been drawn by religious art and he asserts that art would not demand greater correctness and harmony of features and society could well content itself with the polish of her manners and gravity of bearing. He does notice one thing less gratifying: the expression in her eyes was one of sly curiosity and suspicious reserve (*H*, p. 281).

Helena's expression, a foreshadowing of mystery, disappears after her first three days at the Valle home. The narrator then proceeds to win the other characters' and the reader's affection for Helena by summarizing her adaptability and social gifts. As in the physical description, the array of Helena's social gifts seems idealized. She is not only easy to get along with and intelligent, but she possesses infinite tact and a wide variety of interests to suit the conversational preferences of all (*H*, p. 284).

Sudden mood swings, however, augment the ever-present enigma, and her transformation from solemnity to cheerfulness causes somewhat of a shock to her brother, a reaction designed to forewarn the reader. She becomes jovial, witty, and mischievous, in contrast to the quiet controlled gravity with which she had appeared in the dining room (*H*, p. 283).

Inasmuch as he reveals Helena, the narrator uses a balanced mixture of summary and analysis as well as dialogue. In keeping with the central focus of the story, the dialogues do not reveal very much of Helena and are calculated to augment her unfathomability. After a conversation with Estácio in which Helena philosophizes about fear, the young man is left with a strange impression, a result of Helena's sophistication and her precocious understanding of feelings. Salvador's narration completes her characterization. His desires prevailed over Helena's moral convictions and pride when he overcame her resistance to deceiving Valle's heirs about believing that she was in fact an illegitimate daughter. In so doing, Helena would enjoy a more advantaged social situation than her real father could give her.

Estácio's character is summarized and marked by good qualities including intelligence, a disdain for worldliness, uprightness, gravity, and a sensitive nature. For the most part of the novel, his flaw seems to be an irrational and spontaneous inclination for his sister which is shown progressively by his actions as when he burns a note to Helena's suitor in which the young woman encourages the latter in his matrimonial intentions toward her.

It is clear that *Helena* does not represent technical innovations over the other novels in terms of characterization. In the telling of the story, the manipulation of suspense and mystery do emphasize the greater interaction among the characters themselves. Their conflicts, however, are contingent on situations that diminish their value. Helena's moral being is not as impressive as it might have been if she were really Estácio's sister and had resisted his love. Thus, Machado de Assis's ideal of the morally integrated character falls short.[18] The impossibility of fulfillment through marriage once the truth is known seems to give exaggerated importance to societal conventions while Helena's death is so melodramatic that the reader comes away from the novel with a smile on his lips. It is this confusion of resolutions more than anything else that suggests the idea of parody. Since evidence of Machado de Assis's sincerity in regard to the novel seems to counter this hypothesis, it is not possible to add parody, an element of the later novels, to the area of his preparatory phase. The importance of character in this novel resides in Machado de Assis's showing his personages' passions and temperaments in conflict and in that sense, it is relevant to the continuing development of his art.

IÁIÁ GARCIA

Iáiá Garcia, Machado de Assis's final novel of the early phase, is the best written and best organized of the series.[19] The Brazilian master's concern with character is especially well realized in this novel and as in the preceding novels, analysis reveals a thematic relationship to this element. Like doubt in *Resurrection*, the main theme in *Iáiá Garcia* is closely identified with a principal character and obstructs the fulfillment of love. Estela's pride keeps her from transgressing familial and societal barriers to realize her love for the upper class Jorge. The theme of the marriage of convenience refers to Valéria, Jorge's mother, who prefers to send her son to war rather than to see him marry the refined but lower class Estela, who is her adopted ward. The theme also refers to the marriage Jorge's mother arranges between Estela and Luís Garcia, father of Iáiá.

Time is thematic in *Iáiá Garcia*. Its capacity to heal the heart of its wounds is carefully documented between the date of the beginning of the narrative, October 5, 1866, and its end, 1873, one year after Luís Garcia's death. The novel's chronology is scrupulously dated and follows a pattern of segmentation which refers to the durative time followed by a flashback to fill in events leading up to the occurrence at hand. In the 1866 segment, there are characterizations of Luís Garcia, Raimundo, and Iáiá Garcia as well as elaborations of their life and of Maria das Dores and Luís Garcia's dead wife. The same 1866 segment introduces Valéria Gomes and her son Jorge, refers back to her dead husband, and relates Valéria's desire to send Jorge to the Paraguayan War. Twenty days later, he is about to embark and after his visits to Luís Garcia and Estela, there is a flashback to four months previous to this event. Estela, her father Antunes, and their relationship to Valéria and her dead husband are elaborated as is Jorge's and Estela's mutual passion and Valéria's opposition to it. The pattern of significant events related within specific dates and followed by explicatory flashbacks continues through 1870. In 1867, Jorge writes Luís Garcia of his passion without naming the woman, in 1868, he learns of Estela's marriage to Luís Garcia, and in 1870, Valéria dies and Jorge returns to Rio. A flashback to 1866 then relates the history of Estela's marriage to Luís Garcia. From 1871, when Jorge resumes ties with Luís Garcia, and on, the time segments mentioned are smaller—that night, the next day, the hour of day or night, two weeks later, and so on, and are filled by the reactions of the other characters to Luís Garcia's illness, Jorge's interaction with Luís Garcia, Estela's perturbation at Jorge's presence, Jorge's emotional state, and the actions and attitudes of Procópio Dias in regard to Iáiá, Jorge, and Estela. All the subsequent scenes portray the characters' emotional lives and their ambiguity, such as Jorge's interaction with Iáiá, Estela's attitude and role in the triangle, Procópio Dias's villainy, Iáiá's jealous reaction, Estela's withdrawal after Luís Garcia's death, and Jorge's marriage to Iáiá. The content of the time sequences is highly emotional and follows the pattern of previous novels in this respect. The reader is aware, however, of increasing dexterity in the representation of time. Through the long duration of the characters' emotional involvements, the reader comes to know the subjective nature of time in their lives, a feature of the other novels which was not as well integrated into the analyses and action as it is in *Iáiá Garcia*. Thus, time is effectively merged into an interconnecting network with other themes in the novel and provides a structure for the latter.

Unlike his counterparts in the first two novels, the narrator of *Iáiá Garcia* tells us that it is the book itself that will narrate the story. Like *Helena*'s narrator, *Iáiá Garcia*'s is relatively unobtrusive. When he does appear, he anticipates the reader's company: "Before entering, let us find out who the dwellers were" (*IG*, p. 22). He clarifies his speculations for the benefit of the reader while attending to his duties of characterization. He shows Estela much perturbed about her past emotional involvement as she goes to the window and shakes her head. He speculates that it is her hidden past that has come back to cause her heart to chafe at the bit. He shows Estela smothering these impulses, but they continue to appear. When she returns to her chair, her husband had noticed nothing and continued to read his paper (*IG*, pp. 86-87). This scene gives the reader insight into the state of Estela's heart and to her conflicts many years after the events that inspired them.

The narrator shares his omniscience with the reader and knows everything about his personages which their fellows may not, as when Valéria lies to Luís Garcia about her real reasons for sending Jorge to Paraguay. The characters are sometimes self-deceived, as when Procópio Dias wonders if Jorge's reserve is due to causes other than the one he suspects, that the latter is also a candidate for Iáiá's love. Luís Garcia does not know Jorge's whole story but only one side of it. He is in ignorance of Estela's role. Estela wonders if he suspects, however, and is perturbed by the reading of Jorge's letter of 1867 to Luís as we saw above. Iáiá's acuity penetrates Estela's secret. Mutual suspicion between the two women increaces as Estela becomes aware of her stepdaughter as rival for Jorge's love. Estela is irritated at the growing intimacy of the couple, as when Iáiá begins to study English with Jorge, but she is perceptive enough to know when her stepdaughter has triumphed.

Iáiá constantly questions Estela's reactions—a means of informing the reader and characterizing. Her demand that Estela swear she doesn't love Jorge shows her stepmother evading the question while adding yet another facet to the complexity of her character. The narrator reveals Iáiá's motive for the conquering of Jorge, the preservation of domestic harmony, but informs the reader that she had also conquered herself and really loved him. Jorge's doubts and conjectures about Iáiá take the form of speculating as to why she dislikes him at first and later wondering if she is using some kind of strategy to dissimulate her love for him. Jorge, Estela, and Iáiá all have imperfect knowledge of each other. Thus, Iáiá is suspicious when she sees Jorge and Estela sitting together in the garden and Jorge is mistaken when he thinks Iáiá has broken off their engagement at Estela's instigation. Procópio Dias, Iáiá's other suitor, intuits Jorge's hidden love for Estela and entrusts Iáiá to Jorge in his absence. After two ambiguous scenes, Iáiá reveals her real feelings or lack of them for Procópio to Jorge. Once the relationship between Jorge and Iáiá becomes apparent to him, Procópio plots to destroy the young woman's confidence by revealing Jorge's former love for Estela and poisoning Iáiá's mind. She would be led to believe that the marriage itself was Estela's idea.

The ambiguity, hidden motives, partial knowledge, and speculations among the characters parallel lifelike situations and in this
sense mark what one critic has called Machado de Assis's liberation
from the tradition of romance.[20]

This transition can be seen clearly in Machado de Assis's application of the techniques of characterization. In the drawing of Estela,
they are similar to those of the earlier novels—physical description
and moral summary of the beautiful, austere, and proud Estela.
Clearly, the language of the description indicates that she is the
character of greatest value in the novel. Her beauty shines through
her austerity and her moral traits reveal a self-containment later
reiterated by other means. It is important to note that despite
Estela's attractiveness, she does not receive the idealized treatment
of an Helena out of the tradition of romance (*IG*, p. 25).

The narrator analyzes her innermost feelings. Although she
continues to love Jorge, she dominates her passion out of duty and
self-respect. Her strength is reflected in her solitude in this
endeavor. She has no confidants. Her moral strength subjugated
the love she felt for Jorge. She was aware of what was right and of
her own self-respect. The great moral tempest she had experienced
could be seen beneath the serenity of her face (*IG*, p. 137). She
reveals herself in dialogue with Iáiá as she explains to her stepdaughter the reasons why marriage to Jorge was impossible. Her
pride and self-respect were too great to allow herself to be considered the inferior partner in a misalliance. She rationalizes her
marriage of convenience to Luís Garcia on the grounds that their
temperaments were in accordance in regard to the outside world.
Despite what might be interpreted as the fear to attempt, Estela's
integrity is intact enough for her to recognize her true feelings as
she admits how much Jorge's reappearance and the knowledge of
his letter perturbed her (*IG*, p. 159).

Characterization through contrast distinguishes Estela from her
father, Antunes. While the latter is servile, Estela wears her pride
like a halo and for her, it is a strength. Estela was the opposite of
her father. Her pride was not based on envy or ambition; it was a
precious shield for her (*IG*, p. 27). Estela's character contrasts
sharply with Iáiá Garcia's as well. While her stepdaughter is the
soul of adolescence, Estela is much more subdued. At first, the two
women complement each other. Because of the contrasting person-

alities, the two young women had attracted each other. They perfected each other with their respective characteristics (*IG*, p. 51). The total effect is a successful rendering of a woman whose pride struggles with and dominates a love which she believed would have been repugnant to familial values as well as to those of society.

Iáiá's characterization is an outline comparing her movements to those of a bird: "Thus she was Iáiá Garcia. She was tall, slender and mischievous; she possessed the quick and unpredictable movements of the swallow" (*IG*, p. 5). Gesture and facial expressions characterize her emotional life as in the following passage: "Iáiá had risen, taken him by the hand and led him to the window. The discomfiture was visible in her features; her eyes shone with impatience, while her words seemed fearful and recalcitrant" (*IG*, p. 149). The use of dream to express Iáiá's inner life is an innovation in Machado de Assis's craft of the novel. As in life outside fiction, the dream represents anxieties and fears about waking preoccupations. Here, Iáiá's fear that Estela still loves Jorge is expressed literally in the dream. Her anxiety over this matter results in a fall into an abyss in the dream (*IG*, p. 116).

The development of Jorge's initial sketch as a superficial dandy who eventually gains maturity is marked by silent monologue in which he rationalizes his disappointment at Estela's rejection of his declaration of love. His character is so weak that he is convinced that societal conventions should take precedence over true feelings (*IG*, p. 37).

In self-revelation through dialogue, he again reveals his immaturity. Instead of standing up to his mother for his principles and feelings, he agrees to go to war in Paraguay in the knowledge that he will hurt her if anything happens to him. Narrative summary and analysis portray the mature Jorge—capable of taking care of his interests, less preoccupied by unrequited love than before the war, and free from the vices of early youth.

Similar techniques are applied to secondary characters except for one caricature. Procópio Dias's exaggerated physical feature is the series of ridges on his forehead and at one point, Iáiá actually draws a caricature of him. Raimundo, Luís Garcia's black servant, is seen as "an image of gentle manners and the simple joys of love, an element of Brazil's true culture in contrast to the unnatural, barbarous restraints imposed by a European civilization.[21] Lucia

Miguel Pereira bases her view of the persistence of the ethic of the tradition of romance in Iáiá Garcia on the symbolism of personal types in the novel. There are Iáiá the ingenue, Estela the proud, Luís the skeptic, Jorge the capricious, and Procópio Dias the libertine.[22] As we have seen, character drawing is much more complex than Pereira's scheme indicates if we consider the character of Estela, whose internal waxing and waning is in sharp contrast to the symbolism of her personal type, and the skillful and mimetic rendering of the ambiguity marking the relationships among the characters.

The real importance of Machado de Assis's early novels can only be seen in relation to the great works that follow, *Memórias Póstumas de Brás Cubas* (*Epitaph of a Small Winner*), *Quincas Borba* (*Philosopher or Dog?*), *Dom Casmurro*, *Esaú e Jacó* (*Esau & Jacob*), and *Memorial de Aires* (*Counselor Ayres' Memorial*). Nevertheless, we can observe a progression in the art of the early works which encompasses a fundamental concern with character, a constant experimentation with technique, and an iconoclasm which announced literary autonomy from the outset of Machado de Assis's career.

NOTES

1. I have adopted the definitions set up by Wayne Booth in his *Rhetoric of Fiction* (Chicago and London: University of Chicago Press, 1961) regarding the relationships among author, implied author, narrator, characters, and reader.

2. "The true author of the narrative is not only the one who recounts it but also, and sometimes even more so, the one who listens to it. And he is not necessarily the only one to whom it is addressed: there is always somebody else listening." Gérard Genette, *Figures III* (Paris: Editions du Seuil, 1972), p. 267.

3. José Aderaldo Castello, *Realidade e Ilusão em Machado de Assis* (São Paulo: Companhia Editora Nacional, 1969), p. 98.

4. E. M. Forster, op. cit., p. 47.

5. For a fuller discussion of this point, see Machado de Assis's essay on "Eça de Queiroz: O Primo Basílio," op. cit., p. 903.

6. Castello, op. cit., p. 99.

7. Ibid.

8. Machado de Assis, "J. M. de Macedo: O Culto do Dever," op. cit., p. 847.

9. Machado de Assis, *Memorial de Aires*, Vol. I, p. 1153.

10. Harvey, op. cit., p. 142.

11. José Baretto Filho, *Introdução a Machado de Assis* (Rio de Janeiro: Livraria Agir Editora, 1947), pp. 112, 115.

12.

> There are two ways of deviating from that mixed mode of epic narration: one, which may be called the romantic-ironic, deliberately magnifies the role of the narrator, delights in violating any possible illusion that this is 'life' and not 'art,' emphasizes the written literary character of the book. The founder of the line is Sterne, especially in *Tristram Shandy* and Gogol in Russia. *Tristram* might be called a novel about novel-writing, as might Gide's *Les Faux-Monnayeurs* and its derivative, [Huxley's] *Point Counter Point*. Thackeray's much-censured management of *Vanity Fair*—his constant reminder that these characters are puppets he has manufactured—is doubtless a species of this literary irony: literature reminding itself that it is but literature. [René Wellek and Austin Warren, *Theory of Literature*, 3rd ed. (New York: A Harvest Book, Harcourt, Brace and World, Inc., 1956), p. 223.]

13. Machado de Assis, "A Semana," *Crônica*, Vol. III, p. 563.

14. Maria Luisa Nunes, "Machado de Assis's Theory of the Novel," *Latin American Literary Review*, Vol. 4, No. 7 (Fall-Winter 1975).

15. Machado de Assis, *Helena*, Vol. I, p. 270. Nevertheless, other critics have interpreted this work as a mixture of elements. "If the story has a romance background, Machado spiced it with the satire which would come to identify the great fictional work of his maturity." Hélio Pólvera, "Preface," to Machado de Assis, *Helena* (Rio de Janeiro: MEC-Civilização Brasileira, 1975), p. 13.

16. Emir Rodriguez Monegal, conversation with author, Winter, 1975.

17. Helen Caldwell, *Machado de Assis, the Brazilian Master and His Novels* (Berkeley, Los Angeles, and London: University of California Press, 1970), p. 49.

18. Ibid., p. 52.

19. Barreto Filho, op. cit., p. 116.

20. Lucia Miguel Pereira, *Machado de Assis Estudo Crítico e Biográfico*, 5th ed. (Rio de Janeiro: José Olympio, 1955), p. 183.

21. Caldwell, op. cit., p. 69.

22. Pereira, op. cit., p. 183.

3

A NETWORK OF VALUES: THEME AS REFLECTED IN CHARACTER AND PLOT IN THE LATER NOVELS

A NOVEL'S themes may be viewed as an antecedent to character drawing. Characters carry forward or implement themes through their actions. Henry James stated that "character, in any sense in which we can get at it, is action, and action is plot, and any plot which hangs together, even if it pretend to interest us only in the fashion of a Chinese puzzle, plays upon our emotion, our suspense, by means of personal references. We care for people only in the proportion as we know what people are."[1] In the five later works of Machado de Assis, we can see clearly the relationship among theme, character, and plot. Themes are so closely bound up with character that we have identified the former as a technique of drawing the latter.[2] In this chapter, discussion of themes as reflected in character and plot provides an illustration of their interweaving as well as a global view of the plots of the works.

MEMÓRIAS PÓSTUMAS DE BRÁS CUBAS (EPITAPH OF A SMALL WINNER)

Time and egotism or self-love are interrelated and equally important themes in *Epitaph of a Small Winner* (1881). The latter is the law of the former. Under egotism there are many sub-themes including avarice, love of glory, vanity, ambition, hypocrisy, cruelty, oppression, the transiency of human emotions, and survival of the fittest. All of these are subject to and limited by time which irrevocably leads to death, another of the novel's themes. Within the big death are many smaller deaths—the death of ideals and the rejection of life's goals. Despite this release from the dissimulation, pain, and hypocrisy of life, man's anguished quest is to know the meaning of existence. An echoing sub-theme is death in life or a nullification of the emotions. Love as the choice not taken is, I believe, the answer offered to the mystery of life and death while the narrative process itself is thematic and is the means through which the defunct narrator of *Epitaph of a Small Winner* satirically poses and resolves the problem of life's meaning. Let us look at the network of these themes to see how they constitute the plot of *Epitaph of a Small Winner*.

In its broad outlines, Brás Cubas's first-person narrative is a satire chastizing man's inability to grasp significant values from life and his consequent puzzlement over its meaning. The dead narrator's attempt to regain durative time through affective memory is a paradox in more ways than one. Beyond the obvious contradiction inherent in the idea of time beyond death, Brás has nothing but contempt for himself as a living character whose life he recounts. Death brings freedom from dissimulation, pain, and hypocrisy. Furthermore, as a dead man, his affective memory is emotion-proof. He says he feels nothing beyond the tomb but his response to eulogies made at his funeral contradict this assertion. The dominant aspect of his experience, egotism or self-love, is limited by time, which makes Brás its subject because of the exclusion of love and eventually defeats him. His only consolation is the narrative process which gives him the power to restore the past and make judgments about experience.

At two o'clock on a Friday of August 1869, Brás Cubas died at the age of sixty-four. In a flashback to a few weeks earlier, he describes his idea for a "plaster against melancholy" which was to bring him fame and glory. In a second flashback he traces the genealogy of his family, commenting on his father's vanity in claiming aristocratic ancestors who were, in fact, modest artisans. After further elaboration of his ambitions concerning the plaster, he recalls his illness and two visits by Virgília. Surrounding the memory of their adulterous affair are feelings of self-indulgence, hypocrisy, and the transiency of human passions.

Brás next recounts his final delirium before death during which he confronts nature. She shows him the cyclical regularity of the passage of time, which subsists under the law of egotism or self-preservation and inevitably brings death. He revives from the delirum with the mystery of the meaning of an egotistical existence unsolved.

The next transition takes us back to Brás's birthdate, 1805. From this point in time, he narrates his life chronologically until his death in 1869. His formative years are characterized by the development and gratification of egotism. He is spoiled by a doting father and a weak mother, cruelly torments and oppresses the slaves, and plays tricks on visitors. When his whims were countered as in an episode of 1814 when the conservative Cubas family was celebrating the fall of Napoleon and Brás was deprived of dessert because of Dr. Vilaça's prolixity, he took revenge by later spying on Vilaça and D. Eusébia and revealing to the assembled guests that they had kissed behind a thicket in the garden. Beyond its evocation of mischievousness, the episode is important in setting the scene for the appearance of Eugênia, the "love child" of Vilaça and D. Eusébia.

More concerned with the forms of religion rather than its substance, Brás's Uncle Ildefonso, the canon, does little for the boy's spiritual development. His Uncle John, a military man, has rather dubious mores and is a corrupting influence on Brás. He introduces the adolescent to Marcela, a Spanish courtesan, in 1822, year of Brazil's independence and Brás's first captivity. Although Brás believes he loves Marcela, she is only interested in money. He is despondent when his father interrupts the affair by sending Brás to Coimbra to be educated.

Brás evokes the years spent in Europe by recounting his mediocrity and lack of seriousness as a student, his avarice in the episode of the muleteer, and his witnessing of the birth of romanticism. He returns to Rio upon his mother's death, which he recounts with an absence of emotion.

After the funeral, Brás spends time in Tijuca. His father visits him to propose a marriage of convenience to a young woman named Virgília and an accompanying career as a deputy since her father had political influence. Aggrandizement of the family name is his motive. Brás agrees but before he leaves, he meets Eugênia, the flower of the thicket where Vilaça had given D. Eusébia a kiss in 1814, their "love child," Brás's lame Venus—in short, a symbol of love whom Brás comes very close to loving but rejects because love is in opposition to the goals of self-love—in this instance, his ambitions to become deputy. Brás returns to the city to live out his egotistical existence, but he does not marry Virgília and become deputy as a result of the interaction of human vices. Upon meeting the now wasted but still avaricious Marcela, he questions the values of his first amorous experience and imagines Virgília similarly afflicted by time and disease. Perceiving his aversion, Virgília abandons Brás to marry Lobo Neves, an action that is another manifestation of self-love. Lobo Neves promised her a title. The disappointment of Brás's father at his son's failure brings about the death of the older Cubas. As in the recounting of the death of his mother, Brás nullifies emotion in relating that of his father. He again shows his avarice in wrangling over the inheritance with his sister, Sabina, and her husband, Cotrim.

The years go by uneventfully until 1842 when Luís Dutra, an aspiring poet whose self-confidence Brás cruelly undermines out of a desire to increase the young man's self-doubt and to defeat him, announces that his cousin Virgília is back in town. Brás and Virgília embark on an affair which brings only satiety and is an exercise in egotistical self-gratification for both. Although he subsequently desires to marry Nhã-lóló and have children, she dies along with that particular goal. Brás finally becomes a rather ineffectual deputy, but he does not realize his aim of becoming minister. His self-seeking existence is given philosophical justification by Quincas Borba's *humanitismo*, a parody of Comte's positivism. Brás founds an opposition journal which his sister and brother-in-law disclaim, a demonstration of the absence of loyalty or love and of the survival of the fittest. By 1869, year of his own death, Brás has witnessed the deaths of D. Plácida, the woman who provided the front for his rendezvous with Virgília, Lobo Neves, Marcela, and Quincas Borba. Although he has conceived of the idea for the plaster, he does not realize it. Nevertheless, he believes he has finished life a small winner. He has not left the legacy of human misery to any living creature. His meeting with Eugênia at the end of his narration seems to corroborate the thesis of her significance as a love symbol. She has suffered in life from love and lameness but she forces him to treat her with respect. Brás's inability to sacrifice and suffer for love, truth, and dignity points to his rejection of the values that would have given meaning to his existence.

QUINCAS BORBA (PHILOSOPHER OR DOG?)

As in *Epitaph of a Small Winner*, self-love is a dominant theme in *Philosopher or Dog?* (1891). Its sub-themes are also similar to those of the previous novel—vanity, narcissism, social climbing, and cruelty. The sub-themes of madness, an equally important theme, are guilt, ambiguity, jealousy, suspicion, and delusion, all of which are exacerbated by the values of an egotistical society. Interrelated themes are illusion versus reality, man as an instrument of man or exploitation, sensuality versus spirituality, and destiny versus freedom. Counterpoised to all of these is love. The thematic structure of *Philosopher or Dog?* thus mirrors that of *Epitaph of a Small Winner* to a certain extent. By tracing its plot, we see the interweaving of *Philosopher or Dog?*'s themes and their relationship to character.

Madness and self-love make their appearance early in the novel. The mad philosopher of egotism and survival of the fittest, Quincas Borba, dies in 1869, the year of Brás Cubas's death. His universal inheritor is Rubião, a former school master from Barbacena, Minas Gerais. In addition to its capital, the legacy includes Quincas Borba's madness, his philosophy of egotism, and his dog, also named Quincas Borba. Thematically, the inheritance determines Rubião's destiny and precludes freedom. He becomes the victim of money, the egotistical behavior it inspires, and the guilt he feels as a result of acquiring it, all of which culminate in madness. In contrast, the dog, Quincas Borba, is one of the two characters in the novel to understand love. His loyalty and fulfillment in the relationship to his master are the opposing values to those of a society dominated by self-love.

After Rubião has inherited from Quincas Borba, he debates whether he should stay in Barbacena and be brilliant where he had been a nobody or go to the Court (Rio de Janeiro) with all its dazzling attractions. He chooses Rio. On the train, he meets Palha and his beautiful wife, Sofia. Palha begins a systematic exploitation of Rubião upon learning that the *mineiro* (native of Minas Gerais) is a wealthy capitalist. His wife, for whom Rubião develops a passionate attachment, exploits Rubião in a different manner. Rubião becomes the victim of illusion in his fantasies of an adulterous affair with Sofia. The reality is that she continues to tolerate him after he has made a declaration of love to her out of obedience to her husband who was in debt to Rubião and hoped to exploit him further. Within this *modus vivendi*, Sofia's narcissism is fed by Rubião's adulation but this is not the only way in which she exploits him. Because she neither encourages or discourages him, Rubião continues to nourish his fantasy and shower its object, Sofia, with expensive presents.

Underlying Rubião's illusion is the ambiguity resulting from a misinterpretation of other people's motives, as when he imagines that a box of strawberries sent by Sofia is an invitation to adultery. In fact, her husband had dictated the note accompanying it. Another example of ambiguity is Rubião's inability to perceive Major Siqueira's ironic commentary on the story Sofia invents in order to dissimulate when Rubião has been declaring his love to her and the Major comes upon them in the garden. The theme of sensuality versus spirituality is clearly drawn in the former scene. Although Rubião speaks in poetic images, his sensuality gives the tone to the interview.

Palha and Sofia are not the only ones to exploit Rubião. Camacho, a second-rate politician, does the same. He brings out the worst in Rubião, vanity, in his publication of the *mineiro*'s disinterested act of saving a child, Deolindo, from being run over. As he rereads the account, Rubião becomes increasingly more inflated with himself.

If Rubião is the victim of Sofia's exploitation particularly in the form of her narcissism, she in turn is the victim of Carlos Maria's. This young man declares his love for Sofia, an invitation to an affair which Palha's wife mentally accepts, but he does not follow through. Rubião's suspicion and jealousy are provoked by Carlos Maria's attentions to Sofia but are allayed when he learns that the young man will marry Maria Benedita, Sofia's cousin. A victim of her mother's egotism, Maria Benedita has admired Carlos Maria from afar. She misinterprets Sofia's motives in imagining that her cousin wishes to marry her off to Carlos Maria. In reality, Sofia and Palha thought of marrying her to Rubião. Carlos Maria's narcissism is gratified to the point of his marrying Maria Benedita upon learning of her silent love and admiration from his cousin, Fernanda.

Despite Carlos Maria's affront to Sofia's self-love, she and her husband continue their social climbing at the expense of Rubião who becomes more involved in guilt, first over his inheritance and next, over his adulterous desires, ambiguity, and delusions of grandeur until January of 1870 when he imagines himself to be Napoleon III, Emperor of the French.

After Rubião's madness becomes known, his exploiters manifest their cruelty toward him through their indifference to his plight. Now that he has served their egotistical needs, they no longer care about him. The child whose life he saved, Deolindo, joins other children in a street gang tormenting the madman. The one exception to this cruelty is Fernanda, Carlos Maria's cousin. She is a sanguine, good-humored, generous person who, like the dog Quincas Borba, understands love. She is content in a conjugal relationship with a man who loves his work as much or more than he loves her. Her sympathy for the melancholy Maria Benedita results in the realization of the latter's love for Carlos Maria and her kindness toward Rubião incites the suspicious-minded Dr. Falcão to believe that she was or is in love with the *mineiro*. Although she barely knows Rubião, Fernanda effects treatment of his madness and even attends to the dog, Quincas Borba. Her universal sympathy went out to the animal and he responded positively, a symbolic response of love to love. When Rubião escapes from the asylum and returns to Barbacena in search of his lost equilibrium, Quincas Borba is his faithful companion. Rubião dies raving as he crowns himself with nothing, an illusion of fulfillment. His last words, "to the victor the potatoes," and their allusion to the madness of Quincas Borba's philosophy of self-love and survival of the fittest close a full circle from the date of the philosopher's legacy to Rubião's death. Society's values are the same as Quincas Borba's, mad and egotistical. The subsequent death of the dog, Quincas Borba, is unremarked by the heavenly bodies.

As in *Epitaph of a Small Winner*, man's fulfillment in time is hindered by society's value of self-love. Its motives of avarice, vanity, exploitation, and cruelty combine with the seeds of madness—guilt, ambiguity, and delusion—to counter the realization of love. Like nature in *Epitaph of a Small Winner*, the universe is indifferent to this state of affairs.

DOM CASMURRO

In *Dom Casmurro* (1900) we find some of the themes encountered in *Epitaph of a Small Winner* and *Philosopher or Dog*? combined in a new and original manner. They are brilliantly and tightly woven together into what is commonly thought to be Machado de Assis's masterpiece. Self-love versus selfless love is a reflection of death as opposed to life with its echo of the fear of life and failure. Consequently, doubt is a key theme in the novel and suggests the related theme of illusion versus reality. The obverse of doubt is jealousy which grows to be a monomania leading to a tragic end and culminating in guilt. As in *Epitaph of a Small Winner*, time and the narrative process are thematic in *Dom Casmurro*. The latter is a means of recapturing the former. Character change and destiny versus freedom are ostensibly in contradiciton in *Dom Casmurro* but are actually complementary themes and indicative of a choice not taken. A careful first reading or repeated readings of the novel reveal the ingenious way in which these themes make up plot.

The title *Dom Casmurro* refers to a nickname which has been given to the narrator, Bento Santiago. Although he informs us that the nickname refers to his withdrawn and quiet habits, there is also a suggestion that its meaning is relevant to the narrative process and indicates wrong-headedness. The name change mirrors character change during the course of the narrative as well.

Casmurro's motives for writing his book announce many of its themes. He states that he wishes to tie together the two ends of his life, to restore what was in the present. Like Brás Cubas, Casmurro wishes to recapture time through affective memory. The content of this time is the story he tells but his real motive for telling it is guilt. He wishes to lay to rest the shades that haunt him from the past.

Casmurro narrates that one afternoon in 1857, he, Bento Santiago, son of Dona Glória, a wealthy widow whose household included a brother, Uncle Cosme, a female companion, Cousin Justina, and a client, José Dias, was listening at the door. José Dias was reminding D. Glória of her promise to make Bento a priest and warning her of the danger of the boy's close relationship with the daughter of her neighbors Padua and D. Fortunata, Capitu. As a result of José Dias's insinuation, the childhood friendship blossoms into a love relationship in which the two adolescents, Bento and Capitu, plot to avert the young man's entry into the priesthood.

Bento enters the seminary after having solicited José Dias's assistance to get him out. While there, he becomes friendly with Escobar, a young man whom he admires for his charms, intelligence, and mathematical abilities. Escobar suggests that D. Glória's promise to God can be fulfilled by means of a substitute. Bento is thus freed from the seminary. In the interim, Capitu has won a place in the heart of D. Glória and it is expected that upon Bento's graduation from law school, he will marry her.

Escobar marries a close friend of Capitu, Sancha, a little before Bento marries Capitu in 1865. Escobar and Sancha have a child while Bento and Capitu are childless for two years. Finally, they have a son, Ezekiel. The two couples are very good friends and in 1871, Escobar proposes that they all go to Europe together. At the moment Bento and Sancha are shaking hands, he feels an adulterous desire towards her. The next day, Escobar is drowned. At his wake, Bento notices how much Capitu is affected and his characteristic trait of jealousy is aroused.

Although his son Ezekiel is a mimic and imitates adults, Bento begins to think he sees a resemblance in him to Escobar. His unhappiness and suspicions grow and lead him to thoughts of suicide until he goes to see *Othello* one evening. He learns nothing from Desdemona's innocence except that it is Capitu and not he who should die.

On a Sunday morning, he is about to take poison when Ezekiel comes running in. Capitu appears just as Bento has resisted giving Ezekiel the poison and has told him that he is not his father. He then makes his accusation of adultery against Capitu. She and Ezekiel are subsequently exiled to Switzerland where she dies.

When Ezekiel returns a grown man, Bento believes him to be a reincarnation of his friend, Escobar. Ezekiel dies on an archeological expedition to the Holy Land and by this time, Glória, Uncle Cosme, Cousin Justina, and José Dias are all dead. Casmurro is a solitary middle-aged man left with his doubts, guilt, and unhappiness. This is the story that Casmurro tells but the way in which it is told makes it much richer and more complex.

The narrative process in *Dom Casmurro* is typical of Machado de Assis's incorporation of archaic eighteenth-century techniques in order to bypass those of his own century and anticipate those of the twentieth-century novel. His many appeals to pay attention, read carefully, fill in lacunae, and participate actively, places part of the task of deciphering the meaning of the story on the reader. Bento himself gives hint after hint of the ambiguity, forgetfulness, and by implication, falseness of first-person narratives. Through this method of narration then, we may discern the underlying thematic structure of the story.

Doubt is a critical factor in the web Casmurro weaves. He doubts himself and he doubts others. As he compares himself to the brilliant, charming, masculine Escobar who has sired a child, he doubts himself. As he compares himself to the clever, womanly, self-possessed Capitu, he doubts himself. The person he loved most, Glória, betrayed him by promising him to the priesthood. Here we have the seeds of his destiny which determine his tragic end.

The outgrowth of doubting others and self-doubt is jealousy which becomes a monomania in Bento's life. He is jealous of attention Capitu receives from other men, he is jealous of the sea, he is jealous of the dead. Any illusion he has of betrayal by Capitu and Escobar is consequently highly suspect and probably not a reality. His self-love or the doubt that he is loved by others causes him to reject their love and destroy his own potential for happiness and fulfillment. Casmurro's self-love has been equated with death and the fear of life as opposed to Capitu's love, symbolic of life.[3]

Like many of Machado de Assis's protagonists, Casmurro does not understand love and rejects it to his undoing. He has destroyed his happiness and that of people who loved him whether or not his doubts were well founded. He is left alone at the end of his life, unfulfilled, unhappy, and existing in a living death.

ESÁU E JACÓ (ESAU & JACOB)

The thematic structure of *Esau & Jacob* (1904) is very similar to those of the previous novels. Time in all its dimensions and the changing of a political and social order, the end of the Brazilian Empire, are the pillars of the work. All of its other elements have been present in Machado de Assis's novels from the outset. The narrative process through which the story is told is extremely important and gives us the keys to understanding. Love is closely linked to the human quest for perfection or fulfillment while self-love is equivalent to nonfulfillment and reflects itself in vanity, social climbing, avarice, ambition, and political unscrupulousness.

The first members of the society of *Esau & Jacob* we encounter are Natividade and her sister Perpétua. They are on their way to consult a *cabocla* (backwoods) seeress, Bárbara, the "Pithia of the North," about the destiny of Natividade's twin sons, Pedro and Paulo. Bárbara gratifies Natividade by telling her that the twins will be great men even though they fought in the womb and will fight outside. From this moment on, Natividade's sole ambition is to see the realization of her sons' greatness.

In a flashback to 1869, Natividade's pregnancy is announced. The scene goes back further to the arrival of her husband, Santos, in Rio de Janeiro in 1855. He had risen to become a prominent banker. During the course of his ascent, he hid his modest beginnings by ignoring his poor relatives and became so materialistic and self-inflated that only the most grandiose palace would serve to reflect his status. In 1857, he married Natividade, and in 1870, their sons were born.

During a scene at the spiritist Plácido's residence, Santos encounters Ayres, a diplomat. Removed from the society around him, Ayres's stance is one of philosophical contemplation and a reluctance to involve himself in the passions of other people. He interprets many of the narrator's norms since he and the narrator are one person. Ayres the character thus functions as an aid to the reader in understanding the work.

The twins grow and develop, each systematically taking the

opposite point of view from the other. Paulo wishes to study law and is politically radical while Pedro intends to study medicine and is conservative.

In 1886, Flora makes her first appearance in the novel. She is the fifteen-year-old daughter of the calculating D. Cláudia and Batista whose political ambitions are compared to those of Macbeth and Lady Macbeth. Both Paulo and Pedro come to love Flora, their only point of agreement.

The year after emancipation, 1889, witnesses the monarchy's swan song at the ball of the Ilha Fiscal. On November 15, 1889, there is a revolution by the military and the empire folds. Within the next two years, Deodoro dissolves the national congress and passes the reins of government to Floriano, who reestablishes the congress by annuling Deodoro's decree. On February 24, 1891, there is a new constitution.

At this time, Nóbrega, a nouveau riche who had acquired his first important capital from Natividade as she left the *cabocla* and from the mendicant society of *almas* to which it was destined, courts Flora. She has removed herself from society to stay with Ayres's sister, Rita, because of her quandary over the twins, Pedro and Paulo. She cannot decide which suitor she desires as a husband. She rejects Nóbrega's offer of marriage decisively. Because of his wounded self-esteem, he tells his secretary that she refused him because she is ill. Flora does in fact become seriously ill and dies shortly after. The twins faithfully place flowers on her grave one month later. A year or so from then they become deputies, but Natividade does not witness their ascent to greatness. On her deathbed, she asks them to promise they will be friends. The narrative closes with Ayres's conviction that the twins will always be fighting, as they were from the womb.

As in Machado de Assis's most experimental novels, *Epitaph of a Small Winner* and *Dom Casmurro*, the narrative process is thematic in *Esau & Jacob*. If the reader does not participate fully as he is instructed to do, he will not understand the work. *Esau & Jacob*'s narrator is somewhat cryptic in his signals and veils many of them in allusions to other works of literature. It becomes apparent that *Esau & Jacob* is allegorical. In my view, the meaning of the allegory centers around Flora, a symbol of love and human perfection, while the twins represent the impulses toward justice and peace. Ayres is the spiritual father of the twins and the philosophical contemplator of Flora. On the other hand, the allusion to Dante which serves as an epigraph to the work—"dico che quando l'anima mal nata"—refers to souls which will not fulfill their destiny, in this case the failure of all the society of *Esau & Jacob* to realize itself. Its members are too absorbed by self-love to achieve human perfection.

Although the larger society of *Esau & Jacob* is far from reaching this ideal because of its commitment to self-love, the novel ends with a reference to the flower or Flora, symbol of love or human idealism, prominently displayed in Ayres's buttonhole. The twins, the contradictory political impulses toward peace and justice, will remain as they were in their mother's womb, at war. The conclusion suggests that while man has the untapped but usually distorted potential to realize perfection, he is predestined to live out his inherent contradictions, particularly in the political sphere. The statement is not entirely pessimistic from the point of view of the artist who can detach himself from the struggle and view it from outside its arena thus attaining a kind of immortality through art.

MEMORIAL DE AIRES
(COUNSELOR AYRES' MEMORIAL)

The principal theme of the last of Machado de Assis's novels, *Counselor Ayres' Memorial* (1908), is the narrative process itself or the craft of the novel. Throughout Ayres's diary, there are references to esthetic problems followed by the old diplomat's solutions to them. He discusses symmetry in art, how to achieve novelistic interest, economy of expression, verisimilitude, and freedom versus determinism in art.

Paralleling this emphasis on the craft of the novel is the theme of abolition. Ayres maintains a distance between himself and this subject, first by dissociating himself from all the oppression, cruelty, and ignominy of the institution of slavery. His comment that a personal happiness is worth much more than a public joy (abolition) would again seem to mark distance between his value of self-interest and the social problems associated with slavery. His doubts about the panacea which abolition and even the benefits bestowed on the freedmen represented to his countrymen show

Ayres's attitude to be far ahead of his time rather than simply distant. When the protagonist Fidélia gives her plantation to the freedmen, Ayres ends his speculation as to the preparedness of the former slaves to run a plantation in an ellipsis. Its implication would seem to cast doubts not on the freedmen's capabilities but on the expectations of a capitalistic society which had systematically and oppressively kept them from learning its techniques and now expected them to manage within its norms without training. Absent from Ayres's observations is any reference to the implications of slavery to race relations.

The theme of character change is pertinent to Ayres, the diarist, while love's victory over death refers to several personages and includes the sub-themes of music as a resurrection and sensuality versus spirituality.

Ayres's diary dates from January 9, 1888, and goes through August 27, 1889. A retired diplomat who has had a rootless existence in foreign capitals, including a brief marriage to a woman he did not love and who is now dead, Ayres comes home to Rio de Janeiro to spend his last years. His sister Rita, a widow who has vowed never to remarry as a testimony to her love for her dead husband, is a confidant to the old diplomat but even she takes second place to the paper of his diary. Writing is a need and a means of fulfillment for Ayres.

On the anniversary of his return to Rio, Ayres and Rita go to the cemetery to visit the family graves. There, he sees a beautiful young woman, Fidélia Noronha, whom Rita identifies. Ayres's sister makes a bet with him that he cannot win and marry the widow. His response is to create from this proposition novelistic interest, would the widow Noronha remarry, and to set the stage for his own realization of love. Up until then, he had remained on the fringes of life as an observer. He cites a Shelley poem in declaring to Rita that he cannot give what men call love. The theme of love's victory over death is reflected in both Ayres and Fidélia, the former existing in a state of emotional death and the latter emotionally committed to a dead man.

Through his contacts with Aguiar and Carmo, an old couple whose love and unity shine through their every gesture, Ayres is able to observe and follow the young widow's progression. She and

Carmo are like mother and daughter and because Carmo has never had children, Fidélia becomes a fictitious child for the older woman. Carmo has had another fictitious child, Tristão, who now lives in Portugal. Before Tristão reappears in the story, Ayres learns that Fidélia's marriage mirrored the story of Romeo and Juliet. Their families were political enemies and when the young couple fell in love, they were strenuously opposed by their fathers who disowned them when they married. A year later, Eduardo, Fidélia's husband, died and since that time, she remained devoted to his memory and unreconciled with her father. The reconciliation was slow in taking place and didn't occur until Santa Pia, Fidélia's father, was on his deathbed.

Although the diarist observes that Fidélia's admirer, Osório, has no luck with the widow, Ayres's fantasies about the beautiful young woman persist. His admiration, however, follows a trajectory from physical attraction through an appreciation for her spirituality.

After Santa Pia's death and the arrival of Tristão, Ayres follows the widow's resurrection through music—she plays at Tristão's request after he has played—and watches the growth of Tristão's love for Fidélia, her correspondence to it, and their subsequent engagement and marriage.

Aguiar and Carmo are the soul of conjugal love and the love shared among them and their fictitious children, Fidélia and Tristão, brings about a transformation in Ayres. He is now able to give what men call love and thus reflects the theme of love's victory over death. Fidélia's love for Tristão is a continuation of her love for her first husband and is another aspect of this victory. The young couple depart for Europe leaving Aguiar and Carmo, whom Ayres observes from a distance as they sit together looking at each other. Nostalgia (*saudade*) for themselves is their consolation.

Most critics agree that the portrait of Carmo in *Counselor Ayres' Memorial* is that of Carolina, Machado de Assis's wife. The work is an eloquent testimony to conjugal love. Whether or not Aguiar or Ayres represents Machado de Assis's values and person in part, the important assumptions about the author to be extracted from the work reside in its major themes. Machado de Assis was first and foremost an artist. His concern for the creative process may be seen throughout his works. His unique identity as an artist is the one he wished to be recognized. It is perhaps this desire which made him shy away from what has interested many of his critics, the social role of the nonwhite writer in a slave-owning society. Nevertheless, his impulse towards social justice can be seen in many of his works. The roots of oppression and exploitation are to be found in another of his major themes, self-love or egotism. If man wishes to achieve fulfillment and to correct social ills, he must realize love both in a platonic and a personal way but in both cases, his starting point should be himself. *Counselor Ayres' Memorial* may be seen as a final comment on Machado de Assis's artistic production and a further illumination of his world view. Art and the values he expressed through it constituted the meaning of his existence.

NOTES

1. In his article, "Les Homes-Récits," in *Poétique de la Prose* (Paris: Editions du Seuil, 1971), Tzvetan Todorov challenges James's statement that there is no character outside the action or action independent of character and its corollary: if the two are indissolubly tied together, one is more important than the other: the characters, that is, psychology. Every story is a description of characters. Todorov comments:

> Il est rare qu'on observe un cas si pur d égocentrisme qui se prend pour de l'universalisme. Si l'idéal théorique de James était un récit où tout est soumis à la psychologie des personnages, il est dificile d'ignorer l'existence de toute une tendance de la littérature où les actions ne sont pas là pour servir d'illustration au personnage mais où, au contraire, les personnages sont soumis à l'action; et où, d'autre part, le mot 'personnage' signifie tout autre chose qu'une cohérence psychologique ou description de charactère. Cette tendance dont l'Odyssée et le Décaméron, les Mille et Unes Nuits et le Manuscrit trouvé à Saragosse sont quelques une des manifestations les plus célèbres, peut être considérée comme un cas-limite d'a-psychologisme littéraire.

> (It is rare to observe such a pure case of egocentrism that takes itself for universalism. If James's theoretical ideal was a narrative in which all is subordinated to the psychology of the characters, it is difficult to ignore the existence of a great tendency of literature in which actions do not serve as illustrations of the character but, on the contrary, characters are subordinated to action; on the other hand, the word character signifies quite something other than a psycho-

logical coherence or description of character. This tendency of which *The Odyssey* and *The Decameron, The Thousand and One Nights* and the *Saragossa Manuscript* are some of the most famous examples may be considered as a limiting case of a literary a-psychologism.) [P. 78]

Todorov affirms that the character, as James proposes, does not always determine action and every story does not consist of a description of character. What then is character?

> Le personnage, c'est une histoire virtuelle qui est l'histoire de sa vie. Tout nouveau personnage signifie une nouvelle intrigue. Nous sommes dans le royaume des hommes-récits.

> (The character is the virtual story, which is the story of his life. Every new character indicates a new plot. We are in the realm of men-narratives.) [P. 88]

While Todorov's point concerning egocentrism taken for universalism may be well founded, it is clear that Machado de Assis's treatment of theme, character, and action is more compatible with James's theory than with Todorov's exceptions to it. James quote appears in Todorov, p. 85.

2. In his article, "Thématique," in *Théorie de la littérature* (Paris: Editions du Seuil, 1965), B. Tomachevsaki asserts:

> Caractériser un personnage est un procédé qui sert à le reconnaître. On appelle caractéristique d'un personnage le système de motifs qui lui est indissolublement lié. Dans un sens plus restreint, on entend par caractéristique les motifs que définissent la psyché du personnage, son caractére.

> (To characterize a character is a procedure that serves to recognize him. We call a characteristic of a character the system of motifs that are indissolubly attached to him. In a narrower sense, we understand "characteristic" as the motifs that define the psyche of the character, his character.)

It is understood that a motif is the smallest division of a theme.

3. Helen Caldwell, *The Brazilian Othello of Machado de Assis* (Berkeley and Los Angeles: University of California Press, 1960).

4

STORY TELLERS AND CHARACTER: POINT OF VIEW IN THE LATER WORKS

THE NARRATORS

THE analysis of the interchange among implied author, narrator, characters, and reader or point of view in Machado de Assis's first four novels illustrates that the Brazilian master's work does not present a radical dichotomy between the early novels and the last five works as has been commonly thought.[1] Many of the basic features of the former are present in the latter in a more evolved state. The narrators of·*Epitaph of a Small Winner*, *Dom Casmurro*, *Philosopher or Dog?*, *Esau & Jacob*, and *Counselor Ayres' Memorial* exhibit a certain degree of commonality among themselves and continuity from the earlier works as well as reflecting Machado de Assis's experimentalism. Cubas, Santiago, and Ayres of the *Memorial* are narrator-agents or narrators who refer to themselves as "I" and are simultaneously characters. The foreword to *Esau & Jacob* explains that the last of Ayres's journals was a narrative in which Ayres is a character and it is clear that he is the first-person narrator as well. Thus, a pattern similar to that of the other works obtains in *Esau & Jacob*. The only exception to this rule among the later works is *Philosopher or Dog?*.[2] While its narrator is not a character in the novel, he does refer to himself as "I." Dramatization, implicit in any reference to the narrator as "I," is a feature common to all Machado de Assis's narrators.[3] They represent a parody of the conventions of the realist novel and can be traced from his earliest works, although the comic intentions are clearest in *Epitaph of a Small Winner*. Machado de Assis deliberately disrupted illusion and went to the extent of including chapters of dots and exclamation points, so-called useless, unserious, and repeated chapters in which something important is told paralleling Laurence Sterne's juggling with the number captions of his chapters, and inserting black, blank, and even marbled pages in his work.[4] But as Kate Hamburger observes, in *Logik de Dichtung*, "romantic irony, the appearance of the poet, the break of the illusion, might rather emphasize and underline the illusion of fictionality which is the aim of the novelist. The capriccios, the arabesques of the narrator do not necessarily disturb the impression of reality."[5]

The limitations on the narrator's knowledge are defined by his relation to other characters and events. Brás Cubas has a thorough knowledge of the details of his birth and what others said and did at that time but he is careful to let us know that he tells these things as he heard them narrated years later. He cannot tell us about his baptism because he wasn't told about it and is therefore limited by what he observed, experienced, or heard. Quincas Borba's narrator, on the other hand, is omniscient and knows the characters' thoughts: "Rubião was gazing at the bay—it was eight o'clock in the morning. Whoever might have seen him at the window of a large house in Botafogo, thumbs stuck through the cord of his dressing gown, would have believed that he was admiring that piece of quiet water; but I tell you that actually he was thinking of something else" (*PD*, p. 3). He also has the power to clarify his characters' motives. He explains that D. Maria Augusta does not want her daughter to marry because she is selfish and used to being adored by her mother and husband. Now that they were dead, she demanded the same love from her daughters (*PD*, p. 93). Ostensibly there is a discrepancy in *Philosopher or Dog?* in that its narrator refers to *Epitaph of a Small Winner* as *his* narrative, a fact that confuses the identity of the deceased Brás Cubas with that of the omniscient story teller of *Philosopher or Dog?* It is curious that it is not this confusion which has led some critics to identify Brás Cubas as an alter ego of Machado de Assis. Mario Matos, for example, identifies Machado de Assis's central narrator-characters as the author himself, saying that in his novels:

> the center is the position of his mind. Consequently, the central personage is always auto-biographical. It is a pretext for the agility of mental gymnastics. He finds the secondary figures of the novel in reality, in the observation of the world. They are flagrant, they are alive, they are perpetual. They represent the great creations of Machado. Not so the principal figures who are somewhat chimerical. Chimerical but free and assured.

> That is the reason why the novels written in the first person, the stories and the essays are more spontaneous and natural. The ease of wit shows itself freely and the author, touched by his mercurial temperament, by his suspensive and circumstantial genius, can discourse at will.[6]

In fact, the distances between author, his idealization, implied author, and narrator are often very great. The discrepancy can perhaps be attributed to Machado de Assis's use of "romantic irony," or the parody of realism in which the narrators make an issue of their presence.

Dom Casmurro's knowledge is limited by the extreme subjectivity of his observations, experience, and interpretations (a point discussed more fully below) while the narrator of *Esau & Jacob* has a complete knowledge of events that took place outside of his presence, such as the details of Natividade's visit to the *cabocla*. His entries into the characters' thoughts qualify him as omniscient: "Natividade's thoughts ran on the *cabocla* of the Castello, on the prophecy of greatness and the message of the fighting. She again recalled that, really, her pregnancy had not been easy; but, in the end, there remained only the glorious destiny, the greatness" (*EJ*, p. 15). He does not seem concerned about telling us how he knows facts about other characters. His often-reiterated goal is to be understood by the reader, a Machadean clue which warns us that understanding is particularly challenging in *Esau & Jacob*: "If I convey a false impression, I do not do so intentionally. It is true, the words did not come forth like this, grammatical and well enunciated, neither those in the feeble voice nor those in the less feeble: they all made a humming in the ears of his conscience. I translated them into spoken language in order to be understood by those who read me" (*EJ*, p. 14). The final work, *Counselor Ayres' Memorial*, is a first-person diary but its narrator's knowledge of events and characters is filtered through a literary prism. It constitutes a guide to creative writing.

The commonality of Machado de Assis's later narrators is underscored by the fact that they are, for the most part, off-center spectators far removed from human passions and emotions. They are the inheritors of Félix's psychological aberration, the incapacity to live through love. The final five works illustrate a constant exploration of this legacy and take us from the testimony of a defunct author through the resurrection of Ayres in the *Memorial*.

Epitaph of a Small Winner presents us with a dead narrator and a living reader. In the discussion of form—that of a Sterne or a Xavier de Maistre—a disdain for the reader: "Moreover, solemn people will find in the book an aspect of pure romance, while frivolous folk will not find in it the sort of romance to which they have become accustomed; thus it is and will remain, disrespected by the solemn and unloved by the frivolous, the two great pillars of public opinion" (*ESW*, p. 17); in the parody of long prologues: "The best prologue is the one that has the least matter or that presents it most briefly, even to the point of obscurity" (*ESW*, p. 17); and in the assertion that the process of the work is not important when its very mentioning indicates that it is, we are immediately aware of the distance between narrator and reader who should be on his guard. Although he is dead, Brás Cubas knows what people said at his funeral and has feelings about those who praised him (*ESW*, p. 20). His teasing ways with the reader—"Have patience! In a little while

I shall reveal the identify of the third lady" (*ESW*, p. 20)—undercut the seriousness of a literal death but then, he is not a dead author but an author who is dead for whom the grave was another cradle. While Brás Cubas's declaration that as a dead man immune to the opinions of others he can be completely frank and confess his mediocrity, his dishonesty on this point is patent since he felt something upon hearing his own funeral eulogies. Brás himself asks the reader to make judgments and presumably to question his value system as he mitigates his avowedly selfish motives with the cloak of his candidness as a dead man.

Brás Cubas's quest for power and glory precludes the value of love and this is emphasized by his lack of emotion in relating his father's death, a summary to which is juxtaposed a scene of avarice among the inheritors of Cubas senior (*ESW*, p. 97). Like the defunct Brás Cubas's evocation of himself as a character, Casmurro is emotionally dead and is well aware that he himself is missing: "Well, sir, I did not succeed in putting back together what had been nor what I had been. If the face is the same, the expression is different. If it were only the others that were missing, no matter. A man consoles himself more or less for those he has lost, but I myself am missing, and this lack is essential" (*DC*, p. 5).

The role of *Esau & Jacob*'s narrator is somewhat more complicated. Ayres the narrator is quite distant from Ayres the character. He describes the latter from a third-person perspective and inserts quotations from the character's diary within the narration. There is constant interplay among Ayres-narrator, Ayres-character, and the reader: "This was Ayres' conclusion, as one may read it in the Memorial. This will be the reader's, if he cares to conclude. Note that I have spared him Ayres' work; this time I did not oblige him to find out everything for himself as he has been obliged to do on other occasions. For, the attentive, truly ruminative reader has four stomachs in his brain, and through these he passes and repasses the actions and events, until he deduces the truth which was, or seemed to be, hidden" (*EJ*, p. 142). The symbolism of Ayres's role is not only in his double function of narration, but in his profession, that of a cosmopolitan diplomat who is an arbiter among nations and men but who does not share in their passion. Ayres of the *Memorial* is the only one of Machado de Assis's narrators to come full circle. Although he starts off-center quoting the Shelley poem in which he says he cannot give what men call love, he discovers himself through love and comes to life in his old age (*CAM*, p. 83). All of Machado de Assis's later narrators share in their oblique vantage points, but considered as a group show a progression in that the last of them is able to realize love. Machado de Assis's artistry in each individual work shows itself not only in the renovation of eighteenth-century techniques but in the skilled use of such ancient modes as satire and allegory and in the experimentalism of the unreliable narration of *Dom Casmurro*, contemporary with Henry James's literary innovations and considerably before it became a common process of twentieth-century literature.

The final feature Machado de Assis's narrators share is their propensity to commentary, an integral part of the dramatic structure of each work. The theory of the rolling balls in *Epitaph of a Small Winner* points to the theme of the interrelated effects of human vices, while in *Philosopher or Dog?* tears and laughter are said to constitute universal perfection, an ironic observation on the equilibrium of life and its absurdity for the sentient.[7] The digressions in *Dom Casmurro* often function as a key to the narrator's unreliability as when he tells us that his book has lacunae which must be filled in as he does with books he reads (*DC*, p. 120). In *Esau & Jacob*, all the varieties of commentary found in the previous works—narrator's intentions, interventions, direct address to the reader, and consciousness of writing in addition to keys for reading the work as allegory—are present. The most natural environment for this effect is *Counselor Ayres' Memorial*, a diary. Ayres's most interesting asides are on writing and abolition, a topic he treated with great subtlety and more sophistication than many an ardent abolitionist might have projected. The frequency of Machado de Assis's narrators' digressions leads me to conclude that they are not only an integral part of the dramatic structure but in some cases, such as *Epitaph of a Small Winner*, they are much more important than action, a point emphasized by the narrators' contempt for the reader who is only after the story.

SATIRE AND SELF-PARODY

If we were to isolate a central dramatic focus of Machado de Assis's novels, we might choose the act of writing itself. In each of the later novels, the narrator's consciousness of this act is apparent. Northrop Frye calls this a parodistic form of satire. He states:

> *Tristram Shandy* and *Don Juan* illustrate very clearly the constant tendency to self-parody in satiric rhetoric which prevents even the process of writing itself from becoming an over simplified convention or idea. In *Don Juan* we simultaneously read the poem and watch the poet at work writing it; we eavesdrop on his associations, his struggles for rhymes, his tentative and discarded plans, the subjective preferences organizing his choice of details (e.g.: "Her stature tall—I hate a dumpy woman"), his decisions whether to be "serious" or mask himself with humor. All of this and even more is true of *Tristram Shandy*. A deliberate rambling digressiveness is endemic in the narrative technique of satire.[8]

The most obvious example of this self-parody is to be found in *Epitaph of a Small Winner* but it exists in the other novels as well. In *Philosopher or Dog?* the narrator comments on his writing tasks after a passage in which he teases the reader about his willingness to make judgments on the basis of circumstantial evidence: ". . . and yet that was no reason for me to interrupt the episode, or break the continuity of the book" (*PD*, p. 151). In *Dom Casmurro*, Bento doubts his powers of description: "Capitu could not help laughing, a laugh which unfortunately I cannot transcribe" (*DC*, p. 249). Bento's doubts about clarity in writing are more than self-parody. They are symptomatic of his unreliability: ". . . actually, I do not remember with any certainty, and fear that whatever I might say would be obscure" (*DC*, pp. 203-204). In *Counselor Ayres' Memorial*, the narrator's consciousness of writing constitutes a manual of the craft. He does not write down his impressions immediately. Instead, he allows his memory to retain what is worthwhile.

Ayres is concerned with the hypothetical charge by the critics that if he were writing a novel it would lack verisimilitude. He observes that there are too many unexpected symmetries in his narration. He first concludes that a poet once said that the truth can lack verisimilitude. He later returns to the theme and justifies symmetry in art on the grounds that it is a process that imitates life (*CAM*, p. 111).

Casmurro makes the conclusive statement about writing—at fifty, it is an incorrigible habit (*DC*, p. 106-107). As Dirce Cortes Riedel observed, Machado de Assis's novels are about a novelist writing a novel. In this regard, psychological duration must be intense and complex in the reading of the Brazilian artist's output as in *Tristram Shandy*, *Les Faux-Monnayeurs*, and the works of Proust.[9]

Another dimension of authorial self-parody is the narrator's playful ways with the reader. On occasion, he feels like suppressing a chapter or changing the order around, a preoccupation not unmixed with editorial concerns.

> Pardon me, but this chapter ought to have been preceded by another, in which I would have told an incident that occurred a few weeks before, two months after Sancha had gone away. I will write it. I could place it ahead of this one before sending the book to the printer, but it is too great a nuisance to have to change the page numbers. Let it go right here; after that the narration will proceed as it should right to the end. Besides, it is short. [*DC*, p. 237]

In Chapter CIX of *Epitaph of a Small Winner*, the narrator hopes that God will spare him from telling Quincas Borba's history and after declaring that he will not tell it, proceeds to do so in great detail. Much of the narrator's consciousness of literary effects can be classified as *surjustifications*. His excuses to the reader about including too many details or advising the reader to skip passages if he's only interested in the story are a means of defining himself.[10] His love of parody and mild contempt for the reader would seem to underscore his satiric intentions. These are clearly spelled out in his travesties of other literature. Brás Cubas starts *Epitaph of a Small Winner* with his own death and comments, "Moses, who also related his own death, placed it not at the beginning but at the end: a radical difference between this book and the *Pentateuch*" (*ESW*, p. 19). He goes on to satirize both the traditions of romance and naturalism, a reflection of his esthetic autonomy by comparing romanticism to a strong, high-spirited courser like the horse in the old ballads. When the realists found the horse, the romanticists had ridden the poor beast until he was so nearly dead that he finally lay down in the gutter, his flesh eaten away by sores and worms. Out of pity, the naturalists placed him in their novels (*ESW*, p. 50). *Philosopher or Dog's?* narrator expresses a desire to imitate the methods of the great satirists of past centuries—Cervantes, Rabelais, Fielding, and Smollet (*PD*, p. 160).

The consciousness of art as art is always present and finds expression in comparisons of the universe of the novel with other art forms such as theater and opera. Casmurro alludes to the Shakespearean concept of the world as a stage (*DC*, p. 145). Earlier in the same novel, he compares his life to an opera in which he first sang a tender duet, then a trio, and then a quartet, a veritable configuration of his story.

A predictable trait in a self-conscious author is to be preoccupied about publishing. Once again, his intentions seem parodistic: "I arrived. . . . But no; let us not prolong this chapter. Sometimes I forget that I am writing, and the pen moves along, eating up paper, with grave detriment to me as author. For long chapters are better suited to ponderous readers; but we are not an in-folio public, we are an in-12 public, preferring little text, large margins, elegant type, gilt-edged pages, and illustrations . . . especially illustrations. . . . No, let us not prolong the chapter" (*ESW*, pp. 68-69). Brás Cubas's editorial concerns are so great that he goes to the point of inventing a theory of human editions in which the final one is given to the worms. He continues the metaphor of man as a book who despite undergoing various editions is still imperfect. Nevertheless, he is aware that even imperfection has its compensations: "Know, then, that I was already in the fourth edition, revised and amended, but still full of errata and barbarisms; a defect, however, for which there was some compensation in the elegant type and in the rich binding" (*ESW*, p. 89).

The most concentrated occurrence of satirical elements in Machado de Assis's works is in *Epitaph of a Small Winner*. Northrop Frye could well have been writing of this work when he observed that "satire is irony which is structurally close to the comic. The comic struggle of two societies, one normal and the other absurd, is reflected in its double focus of morality and fantasy."[11] In the world of Brás Cubas, the reader recognizes what Frye calls "a grotesque content and an implicit moral standard, the latter being essential in a militant attitude to experience."[12] Although the values of the satirist, in this case Machado de Assis, are difficult to locate, it is clear that between those of the implied author and narrator in *Epitaph of a Small Winner*, there is a tremendous ironic gap. The values of the satirist's idealized self (implied author) shine through in the moral and emotional suffering of the characters.[13] In this sense, Machado de Assis's narrators are emphatically distinct from the author himself and are in no way his alter egos. One episode which established the dichotomy between the real and the ideal world is Brás Cubas's sentimental interlude with the lame girl, Eugênia. Despite the fact that it is this encounter which touches Brás's heart the most, he is afraid to act consistently with his true feelings as opposed to egotistical values. His rationalization is that man is incapable of attaining perfection. The definition of experience is very Humean and Shakespearean—"perceptions which succeed each other with an inconceivable rapidity, and are in perpetual flux and movement." The self therefore can be "nothing but a bundle or collection of different perceptions" without any kind of substantial unity, or structure.[14] Thus, Brás Cubas's identity is very far from possessing the necessary unity of Machado de Assis's ideal of a morally integrated character. Brás could hardly act in accordance with feelings deriving from such a self. He excuses his cynicism by saying that his brain was a stage on which were presented plays of all sorts. In it, all sorts of contradictions were present.

Another important object of satirical attack is man's incapacity to find any meaning in life. Chapter VIII of *Epitaph of a Small Winner* shows folly on the verge of discovering the mystery of life and death, and reason laughing at her absurdity. Indeed, one of Brás's constant preoccupations focuses on this problem. In Chapter LXXV, he questions the value of existence and rejects it in his ratiocinations about the meaning of Dona Plácida's life. If she was born only to suffer, how could a moment of love between a sacristan and his lady justify her existence? (*ESW*, p. 136-137).

Brás's delirium, an allegorical manifestation of satire, compounds the idea of man's impotence and the absurdity of life. The contradiction Brás Cubas finds in himself is an aspiration for eternity which nothing can satisfy, and the absurdity of man's having such a desire.[15] Religious and philosophical systems which propose to validate human experience are ridiculous. The episode of the black butterfly in which Brás kills the insect and then ponders its existence is a satire of man's faith in a concerned deity (*ESW*, p. 82).

The most savage attack is reserved for the philosophy of Quincas Borba's *humanitismo*, that is, Auguste Comte's positivism which postulated the victory of altruism over egotism. According to Barreto Filho, Machado de Assis's sarcasm was applied to naturalist thought in all its variants. He was never satisfied with an artifice in which optimism sought to minimize and make distant from the focus of conscience the fundamental problem of suffering and disharmony in the universe.[16]

To recapitulate, the implied author's values reflect his criticism of the world of the novel as expressed in man's imperfection and his inability to find any meaning in existence. What then constitutes the ideal world against which this one is posited? A perusal of the outward behavior of the inhabitants of the world of Brás Cubas points to their egotism and its manifestations of avarice, venality, hypocrisy, oppression, and the vanity of human actions. The irony of man's condition is that he consistently rejects the one human value which would give his life meaning, love. The ideal world is one in which Brás Cubas's ambitions to become a deputy by making a marriage of convenience would give way to his ability to act on real feelings. Instead, his self-love leads him to be perfectly indifferent to other people's misery as long as his needs are satisfied. The memory of his miserable friend Quincas Borba is quickly forgotten among the fine linens of Virgília's adulterous bed.

He is not alone in his egotism, as the episode of the sea captain's wife illustrates. This man's vanity about his poetry overrides his sorrow on the occasion of his mate's death. Because Brás has praised his poetry, he puts aside his mourning to read his poetry with proper literary emphasis (*ESW*, p. 64).

The self-centered focus of Cubas's existence and its implicit criticism departs from the family's false genealogy and continues through Brás's upbringing as the *menino diabo* (devil child). The end product is the supreme egotist whose avarice is mixed with hypocrisy as in the episode in which he returns a single gold coin he finds, is much praised for his honesty, but keeps the five *contos* he discovers on the beach. Avarice is mixed with venality in Brás's interaction with the muleteer in which the latter saves his life. Mentally, Brás keeps lowering the gratification he will give while venality comes to dominate what was initially a disinterested action on the part of the muleteer. The hypocrisy of Brás's world is satirized in his adulterous affair with Virgília and the implicit contractions between a Catholic Brazilian family — Uncle Ildefonso was a canon—and its outward behavior.

The oppression of the institution of slavery comes in for Machado de Assis's typical subtle attack. While he comments on the perversity of man which leads him to inflict the punishment he has received on others—Prudêncio, Brás's former slave playmate, becomes a slaveowner and whips his slave—he makes it clear who the original oppressor is and where the responsibility lies. In fact, man never learns compassion through his suffering; he simply passes it on to the next victim (*ESW*, p. 129).

The absence of love in the satirical world of Brás Cubas continues into Machado de Assis's later novels as well. The objects of attack are all present in *Philosopher or Dog?* and terminate in meaninglessness, the death of Rubião, raving and crowning himself with nothing. Dom Casmurro's hypocrisy manifests itself in avaricious calculations of his relationship with God while his tragedy is self-inflicted by the rejection of love. Ayres of the *Memorial*, the only narrator who achieves the values of an ideal world, makes a point of dissociating himself from the oppression of other human beings in his comments on the abolition of slavery. He refuses a seat in a carriage that will parade before the palace. He is aware of the communal guilt of the slavocratic society. His final judgment is that it was time to end the institution but its infamy will remain in history and poetry (*CAM*, pp. 44-45).

Satirical elements occur throughout the works of Machado de Assis, but the one true satire is *Epitaph of a Small Winner* in its witty attack on the world of the novel as opposed to an implicit ideal world of love. This was the first of Machado de Assis's experiments and its themes were essentially repeated in *Philosopher or Dog?* The protagonist of this novel, Rubião, is not a narrator-agent as pointed out above, but the story is told by an omniscient narrator from Rubião's perspective. This protagonist shares some of the off-centeredness of the typical Machadean narrator-character in that he is mad. In order to follow Machado de Assis's experimentalism, however, we must go on to his most celebrated novel, *Dom Casmurro*.

Like satire, unreliable narration implies a great ironic distance between the values of the implied author and the narrator. According to Scholes and Kellogg, "some of the most subtle variations on narrational unreliability are attributed to such modern authors as Gide and Ford Madox Ford. In their works, the ironic assurance of a shared viewpoint is deliberately undercut, making the reader not an accomplice to the ironic act but in part, at least, a victim of it."[17] Helen Caldwell's study of *Dom Casmurro* establishes all the evidence for this narrative irony but does not couch the argument within its terminology. Instead, the critic sets out to answer the questions pondered by generations of readers: "Was Capitu guilty of adultery and why was the reader left to decide?" Caldwell asks, "What is the dictionary meaning of Casmurro which the narrator advises us not to verify?" and answers, "An obstinate, moodily stubborn, wrong-headed man."[18] The definition is particularly telling within the concept of unreliability, "a narrative by a profoundly confused, basically self-deceived, or even wrong-headed or vicious reflector."[19]

Most of the case against Dom Casmurro and his attempt to dupe the reader may be found in Caldwell's study, *The Brazilian Othello of Machado de Assis* (1960), but certain unexplored passages of the text of *Dom Casmurro* reflect the very subtle nature of the ironic gap between narrator and reader. In Chapter LXVIII, Casmurro's reference to Montaigne's autobiography is a clear indication of the ambiguity of first-person narratives. Like Montaigne, Casmurro knows that confessional literature can never achieve truth and his wily ways with the reader are much in evidence.

More conclusive than the much documented array of charges against Casmurro's trustworthiness—his lying, sense of inferiority, inconsistency (he has forgotten the song of the sweets pedlar but criticizes Capitu for having done so), hypocrisy about God and money, jealousy, projections of guilt about his own adulterous desires, and willingness to accept circumstantial evidence—is the fact that he will not allow any other point of view in the narrative. After his accusation, Capitu says, "Which one does not leave half said; but now that you have said half, say all" (*DC*, p. 249). He is silent. The logical question to follow is, what is that other half? Casmurro is subsequently afraid that Capitu has gone to his mother's house after mass to win support against his case and when Ezekiel returns grown up, he does not want the others to see him for fear that they will detect a resemblance to him. Casmurro, then, has destroyed his own capacity to participate fully in life through love as well as the happiness of other people. A question more important than the one he asks at the end of the narrative as to whether the Capitu of the Praia da Gloria was within the girl of Mata Cavalos, is whether Casmurro was within the Bentinho of Mata Cavalos—and the answer is tragically yes. If Bento Santiago's narrative is accepted as unreliable, what has previously been thought of as the ambiguity of Machado de Assis's masterpiece can also be viewed as its heralding of the twentieth-century novel and testimony to the Brazilian artist's extremely modern and innovative approaches in the creation of literature.

Esau & Jacob's allegorical aspect, the third of Machado de Assis's experiments, is defined by "a kind of didactic narrative which emphasizes the illustrative meaning of its characters, setting, and action."[20] What Machado de Assis shares with other great allegorists is extraordinary literary learning and linguistic ability.[21] The former feature can be seen clearly in Machado de Assis's intertextuality. His narrator's early references to *The Eumenides* transport the ancient Greek drama's representation of the changing of the old order with its code of blood revenge to one of a radical democracy based on justice to the Rio de Janeiro of the 1880s where another old order was giving way. The continuing literary allusions to Greek lierature define the characteristics of the Brazilian symbols. The politically radical Paulo is the angry son of Peleus while the conservative Pedro is the crafty Odysseus. The most challenging symbol, however, is that of Flora, an indecipherable being according to Ayres. In the following passage, her meaning would seem to reside in man's ever-frustrated quest for perfection rather than in a narrower allegorical figure of the ideal republic as has been suggested:

> Mysterious is the term we might apply to artists that paint without ever finishing the painting. They slap on color, more color, another color, much color, little color, fresh color, and it never seems to them that the tree is a tree or the cottage a cottage. If it's people they're painting, good night! No matter how much the portrait's eyes may speak, such painters always

imagine they don't say anything; and they retouch with so
much patience that some of them die between two eyes, others
kill themselves in despair [*EJ*, p. 85].

Flora's unwillingness to choose either Paulo or Pedro places her
above the mundane considerations of marriage like the virgin
goddess Athena of *The Eumenides* and on a somewhat mystical
plane where she is often completely absorbed by music. Her
affinity to Athena is reflected by her strong sense of justice as well.
In Paulo's absence, she defends him to Pedro and vice versa. She is
also specifically referred to as a goddess. Unlike her very prag-
matically political parents, her realm is of an ideal and unattainable
world. Machado de Assis's allegory is mixed with satirical elements
in that the rest of this fictional world is filled by the same values of
his previous novels—egotism, love of glory, avarice, ambition, and
hypocrisy. Ayres is outside of this world by virtue of his profession
of diplomat and his role as spectator-narrator. Like other
Machadean narrators, he seems to be saying that whatever the form
of the political order or system, it will not achieve the values of an
ideal world while men persist in pursuing their motives of self-love.

The linguistic component of Machado de Assis's allegory assists
the reader in understanding the narrator's intentions. He says he
speaks in images and drops hint after hint of the responsibility of
the reader in the task of deciphering (*EJ*, pp. 102-103). Like his
other experimental forms, Machado de Assis's allegory relies
heavily on reader collaboration in order to be understood. The
success of his satirical, unreliable, and allegorical novels is posited
on the reader's having taken the narrators' advice to read
attentively.

The implied author's creation, the reader, functions as a bridge
between the narrator and the real reader, that is, the person who
picks up the book as distinguished from the one involved in the
narrative process, and he becomes a spokesman for the morality of
the work. His importance depends on whether the author is
interested by narrative techniques.[22] This is most certainly the case
with Machado de Assis and throughout his works, we see the
evidence of a highly developed relationship between narrator and
reader: The most obvious signs are his direct addresses to the
reader.[23] In the eighteenth century from which Machado de Assis

borrows many of his techniques, the frequent occurrence of direct addresses to the reader was an indication of the author's need of immediate cooperation from the reader in presenting innovations to the novel.[24] At times, Machado de Assis's narrator calls the reader "my friend reader" (*leitor meu amigo*), as he comments on his narrative technique. He could have been paraphrasing Fielding at various junctures in his texts. The English artist said that "reading his book is like a journey during which the occasional reflections of the author are to be regarded as resting places which will give the reader the chance to think back over what has happened so far."[25] The Brazilian master calls his pause a preparation for things to come (*DC*, p. 116).

Elsewhere, he anticipates the reader's reaction to events in the novel, one of the many steps in winning sympathy for the narrator. In the eighteenth-century context, it is the reader's reactions that bring out the meaning of the novel.[26] Hearing only Casmurro's side of the story, however, creates more of an obstacle for the reader in arriving at that meaning and presents a real test of his participation. When the same narrator is attempting to give proof of his honesty, he directs his confession specifically to the reader. Here, he hopes to minimize his guilt by opposing it to his candidness with the reader. This is part of his aim to engage the moral judgment of the reader on his side (*DC*, p. 136).

In *Epitaph of a Small Winner*, the narrator's prediction of the reader's reaction is the point of departure for his rationalizations about his lack of depth, but in this novel a great deal of the narrator's speculations about the reader's response is based on the assumption that the latter will often find himself inadvertently identifying with the egotism of Brás Cubas and the other inhabitants of his world (*ESW*, p. 164).

The Machadean narrator is often quite precise in his relationships to the readers. Virgília is a reader of Brás Cubas who assures her of his sincerity, a means of characterizing himself and an indication of the different time levels in the novel, that is, that of Brás the character as opposed to that of Brás the defunct author (*ESW*, p. 77).

One of Casmurro's readers is a priest of whom he asks pardon for his hypocritical ways with God, an area of moral judgment in the work. Casmurro never pays his debts of prayers to God for favors rendered and if his wily ways with God are an indication of his essence, the reader should beware (*DC*, p. 138). For Ayres of the *Memorial*, the reader is replaced by paper: "I would not say this to anyone, face to face, except to you, paper, to you who receive me with patience, and occasionally with satisfaction, to you, old friend, to you I tell these things and shall tell them even though it cost me dear, and it does not cost me a thing" (*CAM*, p. 137). Like the reader, the paper of Ayres's diary is a friend in whom the narrator confides to the exclusion of other readers, but its function here is to receive ironic commentary on moral questions, in this case, the nature of appearance and reality: "This, yes, dear paper, this you may record, because it is the pure, inside truth, and no one reads us. If someone did read us, he would think me evil, and nothing is lost by appearing to be evil; one gains almost as much as by actually being so" (*CAM*, p. 42).

Beyond the defined role of the reader cited above, he must also fulfill another function in the novels of Machado de Assis. He must collaborate in the creative process. "The reader must participate actively in bringing out the meaning and this participation is an essential precondition for communication between the author and the reader.[27] The narrator repeatedly admonishes the reader to read attentively. Dom Casmurro lets the reader know that there are lacunae in his work that must be completed. Here again Machado de Assis was borrowing from the eighteenth century. "The reader is shown the event and the outer appearance, but he is invited, almost exhorted, to penetrate behind that appearance, and finally to thrust it aside altogether, by conceiving the idea within. This is an almost direct statement of the role of the reader in the novel. From the given material he must construct his own conception of the reality and hence of the meaning of the text":[28] "The fact is, everything is to be found outside a book that has gaps, gentle reader. This is the way I fill in other men's lacunae; in the same way you may fill in mine" (*DC*, p. 120). Brás Cubas warns the reader that if he does not retain cetain facts, he will never penetrate the narrator's subtlety (*ESW*, p. 168).

If the typical Machadean narrator is very strict about reader involvement, he sometimes goes out of his way to assist the reader in understanding, as in the passage on the epigraph of *Esau & Jacob*. Once the allusion to Dante has been traced, it appears that the content of this opening to the reader functions as a basis for making moral judgments on the work. With the glasses given by the narrator, the reader is better able to perceive the foreshadowing of the lack of fulfillment for the entire society of *Esau & Jacob* (*EJ*, p. 41). The expectation that the reader will take an active part in the narrative process is apparent in Chapter LXXXVI of *Epitaph of a Small Winner* where he is called upon to decipher Virgília's pregnancy (*ESW*, p. 150).

The narrator of *Esau & Jacob* recognizes that each reader's response is individual and knows that he must be tolerant enough to recognize man's variability. His observation is not without humor if we consider that the expression he refers to reflects the joy of prospective parents who have been childless for over ten years. Its comparison to one of somebody anticipating a dance is a pushing of understatement to its utmost limitations. He tells the reader that he is about to learn about something he should have figured out by now, but he asserts that a certain expression for one person means something else for anothr (*EJ*, pp. 20-21). The reader's involvement is taken for granted when a narrator assumes that the reader has understood.

If the narrator loses patience with the reader or suspects that he is not participating fully, he shows his contempt. The reader is called obtuse for never having entered into the mind of a hatter in one instance, and nescient for not having saved old letters. More serious, however, is the reader's failure to understand. Because of this, he may be left out of experiencing the most subtle sensations of this world. To avoid the reader's exclusion, the narrator of *Dom Casmurro* sometimes repeats things and explains exactly why he does so not without teasing the reader. He admits that Capitu was more of a woman than he was a man and does not apologize for his possible repetitiveness because he believes that some things must be impressed on the soul in this way (*DC*, pp. 62-63).

Brás Cubas is quite irate about having to explain everything. Again, he is preoccupied with the time of the dead Brás Cubas in relation to that of the living character. He explains to the critic that as a dead man, he no longer ages but as he tells each part of his story, he has the emotions corresponding to his age at that time.

Of all Machado de Assis's readers, the lady reader is the object of his narrator's greatest contempt. This aspect of Machado de Assis's novels descends directly from eighteenth-century literature. The lady reader appears to read only for the love interest. She is also afraid of the novel's abysses and the narrator must make special concessions to her.

The most serious accusation against the reader is his willingness to make judgments on the basis of circumstantial evidence. Such a situation is designed in *Philosopher or Dog?* where he discusses the circumstantial events that seem to point to a love tryst between Sofia and Carlos Maria on the Rua da Harmonia in the imagination of Rubião. The narrator attributes calumny to the reader and Rubião for reaching such a conclusion. A similar set of circumstances is the basis for Dom Casmurro's accusation against Capitu.

A milder form of the narrator's contempt is a kind of teasing or playful relationship with the reader. In *Esau & Jacob*, he imagines that the reader's sex will determine whether or not he or she understands. If it doesn't matter, he recommends patience. When the reader is too active in the creative process, she is chastised. Once again, this type of digression seems to be included for humorous ends and really encourages the reader to do just what she is criticized for doing, that is, participate fully. The narrator claims that he dislikes people who are always figuring things out for themselves. Again he chastises the lady reader and advises her to write her own book if she cannot read quietly from line to line. He permits her to yawn from time to time but asks her to have faith in the narrator of these adventures (*EJ*, p. 72). Impatience seems to be an attribute of Machado de Assis's lady readers and his narrator asks questions in the text on her behalf about whether or not a female character is in love (*PD*, p. 196).

The narrator's playful ways with the reader are a means of characterizing his satirical and comic intentions as well as forming part of the more generalized process of reader collaboration. While he allows the reader access to the implied author's processes of telling the story, Machado de Assis places a great deal of importance on the reader in the narrative process, a reflection of his concern with its techniques.[29] It is the reader's responsibility to complete Machado de Assis's novels in the way indicated by his subtle and oblique perspectives on the subjects.

THE IMPLIED AUTHOR

The implied author's relationship to the characters in Machado de Assis's later novels reflects an ironic gap similar to the one which

distances him from the narrators. Throughout these works, characters act out the values of Machado de Assis's satirical worlds.
Entire populations of his novels are victims of each other in an
absurd existence characterized by irony and ambiguity in which
love is a rare occurrence. Self-love is the norm and is reflected in
vanity, such as that of Natividade in *Esau & Jacob*. Although
happily married, she opposes a possible match between her former
admirer, Ayres, and her recently widowed sister, Perpétua. Carlos
Maria of *Philosopher or Dog?* cultivates self-admiration to the
point of narcissism. As his adoring wife runs her fingers through
his hair, he continues absorbed in his reading. She gradually
withdraws and he continues to read a study about the famous
statue of Narcissus in the Museum of Naples (*PD*, p. 240).

When Machado de Assis's characters are involved in romantic
love, great passions capable of transforming lives, an underlying
hypocrisy is patent. Virgília and Brás Cubas are involved in such a
relationship but she will not leave her husband because she also
loves public consideration while Brás is quick to realize that despite
all its delights, terrors, remorse, and pleasure, their passion is
transient and will end in satiation (*ESW*, pp. 108-109).

In another relationship, Sofia of *Philosopher or Dog?* shows her
hypocrisy in practicing a good action toward Rubião not out of
compassion but out of snobbery. She proposes to be generous to
Rubião because a woman of greater social status than she had
shown interest in the man's predicament. She wanted to be equally
noble and distinguished (*PD*, p. 229).

It is not only in the "love" relationships that hypocrisy prevails.
Lobo Neves, who entered politics out of choice because of the
desires of his family, and because of ambition and vanity, finds it a
totally unfulfilling experience. After this sad and somber
confession to Brás Cubas, he sees some of his political colleagues
and acts as jovial as if he weren't simply playing a role.

Love relations, whether romantic or familial, are entirely super-
seded by material considerations. Avarice and love of gain are
Marcela's main motives, not love for the young Brás Cubas. He, his
sister Sabina, and her husband show the same traits in their dispute
over their father's legacy. Greed is linked with venality in the case
of Cristiano Palha, who virtually sells his wife in order to exploit
Rubião. When Sofia's husband learns of the *mineiro*'s attentions to
Sofia, he does not throw Quincas Borba's inheritor out of the

house because he says he owes him a great deal of money and fully intends to obtain more from the same source.

Self-love exists in more venial forms as well, as in the example of the bank director whose self-esteem had been wounded by his visit to the home of a minister. He himself had behaved in a completely servile manner and had been treated accordingly. At the end of this visit, he was humiliated and vexed with himelf but he was able to recuperate his composure by means of a visit to Palha's house where he played the role the minister of state had played to him in relation to Palha—a classic example of the pecking order.

If man is vain, he is also pusillanimous. After Rubião has gone mad, he is followed on the street by gangs of children. One of these is Deolindo, a little boy whose life Rubião had saved. The child's father recognizes Rubião and wants to help him but is afraid that the children will turn on him. He averts his face and simply comments to his wife that it's sad to lose one's wits.

Brás Cubas's cruelty is psychological. Knowing that Luís Dutra, an aspiring poet, needs reinforcement about his writing, Brás refuses to give it with the intention of increasing the poet's self-doubt. When the poet seeks approval, Brás speaks of all kinds of other things except his poetry. After trying to steer the conversation toward his works unsuccessfully, the poet would leave. Brás's aim was to discourage him and eliminate him as a competitor (*ESW*, pp. 101-102).

The only example of disinterested love in Machado de Assis's satirical world of *Philosopher or Dog?* is that of Fernanda, illustrated by her treatment of the dog, Quincas Borba. "The dog was drawn and held by the all-embracing sympathy that was the essence of this woman, a sympathy so great that it did not hesitate to give of itself and enfold within itself this obscure little misery that was only an animal's. The woman, at sight of the poor creature, felt the same distress she had felt at the thought of the madman, as if both were of the same species; and feeling that her presence brought some comfort to the animal, she did not wish to deprive him of it" (*PD*, p. 263).

The world of Dom Casmurro is suspect because of the narrator's extreme subjectivity, in which José Dias's opportunism, Justina's suspicion and envy, Dona Glória's betrayal of her son by promising him to the priesthood, and finally, the conviction that Capitu has deceived him with Escobar become the prism through which we witness the events of the story. Casmurro, who as Bentinho was admittedly jealous and continued to grow more so, builds the case against a dissimulating Capitu. His proof is his child's resemblance to Escobar, but Ezekiel's tendency to mimicry and Casmurro's monomania of jealousy make it less than convincing.

The world of *Esau & Jacob* symbolizes the vices of the previous novels in terms of their corrosive effect on society and the resulting frustrations of its members. Natividade dreams of greatness for her twin sons, they pursue opposing political doctrines, Santos aims for position and status, Batista, led by his Lady Macbeth of a wife, seeks political success by compromising personal integrity, Nóbrega, money, but none achieves the perfection of fulfillment symbolized by the inaccessible Flora. It is only in the final work, *Counselor Ayres' Memorial*, that the characters realize the values of love shared among each other and focused through the narrator-character, Ayres.

What becomes clear through the study of point of view in the later novels of Machado de Assis is that we are dealing with metaliterature or literature about literature. Narrative self-parody is present throughout and results in irony or distance in the relationships among implied author, narrator, characters, and reader, the basis for Machado de Assis's experiments and innovations.

NOTES

1. One of Machado de Assis's earliest critics, however, recognized the continuity of his work even though he was not wholeheartedly enthusiastic about it: "Machado de Assis's new manner is not in complete antinomy with his past. It is merely the normal development of the good germs he possessed natively into what the new tendency has of value and the normal unfolding of certain innate defects into that which is bad." Sylvio Romero, *Machado de Assis*, 2nd. ed. (Rio de Janeiro: Livraria José Olympio, 1936), p. 25. See also Massaud Moisés, *Temas Brasileiros* (São Paulo: Conselho Estadual de Cultura, Comissão, V, 142 de Literatura, 1964),p. 15.

2. This work is considered by some critics to be a step backward in Machado de Assis's art:

> . . . the book was inferior to the preceding work, not in its power of observation, not in the types, not in its language, but in its atmosphere, in a certain lack of nerve, and of cohesion: it is because

it was not written in the first person. Machado, not much of a colorist or animator whose strong point is in depicting interior lives, states of soul, and subtleties of psychology, was much more effective with direct narrative. [Pereira, op. cit., p. 229]

3. Booth, op. cit., p. 152.

4. René Wellek, *Concepts of Criticism* (New Haven and London: Yale Univesity Press, 1963), p. 250.

5. Quoted by René Wellek in ibid., pp. 250, 251.

6. Mario Matos, *Machado de Assis: O Homem e a Obra* (São Paulo: Companhia Editora Nacional, 1939), pp. 199, 200. See also Augusto Meyer, *Machado de Assis* (Rio de Janeiro: Livraria São José, 1958), p. 17.

7. More than one critic has complained about aspects of *Philosopher or Dog?*'s narration. According to Mario Matos, the commentary in this novel seems an intrusion and what was observed above to be a confusion of two narrators' identities, Matos views as simply a strange way to present a character.

For the reader, reading is the enjoyable absence of the outside world. The reader is transported to a spiritual level, so that the sudden presence of the author is shocking like that of an interruption which surprises us at a moment of abstraction, leading us to a different reality, that of the world. This is what occurs in the pages of this novel. It is a habit of Machado de Assis. [Matos, op. cit., p. 200]

8. Northrop Frye, *The Anatomy of Criticism* (Princeton: Princeton University Press, 1957), p. 234.

9. Dirce Cortes Riedel, *O Tempo no Romance Machadeano* (Rio de Janeiro: Livraria São José, 1959), p. 103.

10. Gerald Prince, "Introduction à l'étude du narrataire," *Poétique*, Vol. 14 (Paris: Editions du Seuil, 1973), p. 185.

11. Frye, op. cit., p. 224.

12. Ibid.

13. Booth, op. cit., p. 73.

14. Hans Meyerhoff, *Time in Literature* (Berkeley and Los Angeles: University of California Press, 1955), p. 32.

15. Barreto Filho, op. cit., p. 135.

16. Barreto Filho, op. cit., p. 137.

17. Robert Scholes and Robert Kellogg, *The Nature of Narrative* (London, Oxford, and New York: Oxford University Press, 1971), p. 264.

18. Caldwell, *Brazilian Othello of Machado de Assis*, p. 2.

19. Booth, op. cit., p. 340.

20. Scholes and Kellogg, op. cit., p. 107.

21. Ibid., p. 108.

22. Prince, op. cit., p. 196.

23. See J. Mattoso Camara's article, "Machado de Assis e as Referências ao Leitor," in *Ensaios Machadianos* (Rio de Janeiro: Livraria Acadêmica, 1962).

24. Wolgang Iser, *The Implied Reader* (Baltimore and London: The Johns Hopkins University Press, 1975), p. 29.

25. Fielding, quoted in ibid., pp. 39, 40.

26. Iser, *op. cit.*, p. 32.

27. Ibid., p. 30.

28. Ibid., p. 40.

29. One Brazilian critic has astutely observed the demands Machado de Assis places on the reader:

> Machado de Assis seemed to write under the eyes of the reader, to attract the latter to him to consult him each time he has to make choices. But let's not make a mistake; if the convocation of the reader is a fact and as an esthetic expedient, favors the narrator's facilitating the task of choice between this and that, a requisite of all art in the final analysis, creating conditions so that the ironic criticism to which Machado de Assis is always disposed becomes more original and subtle, it is certain, on the other hand, that the author plays a game of hide and seek with the reader, obliging him to be constantly on the alert with his attention directed between the lines, his intelligence always poised. [Maria Nazaré Lins Soares, *Machado de Assis e a Analise da Expressão* (Rio de Janeiro: Instituto Nacional do Livro, 1968), p. 68]

5

THE QUEST FOR TIME

A STUDY of time in Machado de Assis's later works runs the risk of being repetitive since this element is the subject of a critical book on three of these novels, but a close examination of time is necessary for establishing a theory of character in the novels.[1] My discussion will touch upon chronological order and rhythm; aspects of these categories such as techniques of acceleration, deceleration, digression, and other discrepancies in relation to the selective processes of memory; the time stacks of narrator, characters, and reader, and significant associations, that is, what does a man or omniscient narrator recount in the reconstruction of his life or that of other people?[2] Each novel is treated separately, with comments on the common features of Machado de Assis's handling of time in the later works.

EPITAPH OF A SMALL WINNER

The first half of the title, *Memórias Póstumas* (posthumous memoirs), gives us a key to its relationship to time and immediately raises a contradiction. Since the eighteenth century, memory has been thought to enable man to "escape the purely momentary and the nothingness that lies in wait for him between moments of existence."³ Presumably, this nothingness obtains for moments beyond existence as well, that is, in death. Brás Cubas's narration is paradoxically a dead man's attempt to regain duration based on affective memory. In recounting the experiences of his life, Brás Cubas relives them and regains time from beyond the tomb. Hence, we are dealing with the "time" of a dead man (time of the narrator) as opposed to the time of the narrative (the events of his life). Throughout his narration, Brás Cubas is naturally concerned with time, the most characteristic mode of human experience according to Kant, but this posthumous preoccupation is more satirical than strictly metaphysical. If we were to take the content of Brás Cubas's narration at face value, we would have to agree that his life was meaningless and the "small balance" he refers to at the end was indeed a positive feature among the many negatives of his existence. In a satirical context, however, his narration may be viewed as a chastisement of society and man's inability to grasp meaningful values in life. For Brás Cubas and others like him, there will never be fulfillment and the passage of time will only accentuate this emptiness. Subjective time as defined in terms of experience is the most important concern in an analysis of the temporal structure of *Epitaph of a Small Winner*, but as in Machado de Assis's earlier works, this aspect is framed by chronometric time which leads us into a discussion of the order of the events of the narrative.⁴

The date on which the narrative begins is two o'clock on a Friday of August 1869. On that day, Brás Cubas who was sixty-four years old, died. In the second chapter, Brás, the first-person narrator-character, goes back a few weeks before his death to describe the idea of the plaster which took hold of his brain one morning. In Chapter III, there is a flashback to the genealogy of his family and in the next chapter, he resumes the narrative of the plaster with various digressions. Chapters V and VI witness Brás's illness and two visits from Virgília two days apart, and in Chapter VII, his delirium takes twenty to thirty minutes of clock time. After a digression on reason and folly in Chapter VIII, he makes "the greatest transition of the book" jumping back to October 20, 1805, the date of his birth. Chapters X through CLX narrate selected events from Brás Cubas's life chronologically and come back to the starting point, his death in 1869, with a reference to the early events of the novel having occurred between the death of Quincas Borba and his own. The narration, therefore, begins and ends with Brás Cubas's death.

The larger of the two time loops described, 1805-1869, includes many specific references to chronometric time. On a Tuesday in March 1806, Brás was baptized. He recounts episodes when he was five and six as well as one marking the first fall of Napoleon in 1814 when he was nine. He then jumps to 1822, date of Brazil's independence and his first personal captivity. The elaboration of this episode is followed by an acceleration of the eight or nine years Brás spends at Coimbra and traveling in Europe where he witnesses the birth of romanticism until his return to Rio upon his mother's death. The next date is 1842, approximately ten or eleven years after his father's death, a period which Brás measured "stretched out in a hammock." Thirteen years later in 1855, Brás has lived through his affair with Virgília, been frustrated in his marital ambitions toward Nhã-lóló, and become a deputy. By the date of Brás's death fourteen years later in 1869, he has not become a minister, he has heard Quincas Borba's philosophy, founded a journal, witnessed the deaths of D. Plácida, Lobo Neves, Marcela, and Quincas Borba, and as narrated in the smaller time loop, he has conceived the idea for the Brás Cubas plaster. Although the plaster does not bring him fame and glory, he believes he has finished life a small winner.

Within the larger measurements of time, there are smaller units—days, weeks, and months which correspond to the sequence of highly emotional events in the narration, usually Brás's amorous adventures. Thus in the relating of his affair with Virgília, he goes to the point of recording a change of feeling between nine and eleven o'clock of the same evening in one instance and is much more scrupulous about marking smaller segments of time than in the less emotionally charged periods of his life.

There are, however, larger rhythms in the narrative made up of the alternation among scene, summary, and iteration. To these, W. J. Harvey would add other rhythmic features which find their correspondence in memory: "Flashbacks, anticipation, digression, sudden accelerations of tempo—all the discrepancies between reading time and contentual time we accept without question because we have an analogue for this in the rich, free play of our own minds over past and future. Memory may be arbitrary and capricious or it may yield to the discipline of deliberate recollections—in either case it affords a basis in reality for the artifice of the novelist.''[5] The narrator-character seems to be in control of the occurrence of summary, scene, iteration, digression, flashback (summary or scene), acceleration or deceleration of time and thus determines the rhythm of the narrative.[6] Lurking behind him, however, is the implied author who is the real organizer of temporal criteria, a point which must be kept in mind in regard to the thesis to be discussed below. The narrator, however, warns us that this book is written leisurely by a man not concerned by the flight of time; it is philosophical, but of a philosophy sometimes austere, sometimes playful, something that neither edifies or destroys, inflames or chills, and it is more than pastime and less than preachment (*ESW*, p. 24). The sluggishness or deceleration of time in the narrative is effected through the many digressions, flashbacks, and the delirium which is curiously speeded up towards its end. The narrator accelerates time by making several large jumps—one over his school days, another up to his adolescence, another over his years at the university and traveling in Europe, and another following his father's death. The period after his affair with Virgília until shortly before his death is vaguely filled by the deaths of other characters as well as the deaths of Brás Cubas's ambitions — to marry, have children, and become a minister. Brás Cubas again comments on the book's rhythm in Chapter LXXI. He fears that it is tedious and smells of the tomb. But the real defect of the book is the reader who wishes to speed on to the end while the book ambles and staggers like a pair of drunks (*ESW*, pp. 131-132). If we turn now to the time stacks of narrator, characters, and reader, we again find contradictions between the "time" of the dead and that of the living.

Brás Cubas clearly judges himself superior to the living. He is careful to establish a distinction between his two selves, the dead narrator and the living character. Whereas the latter was a mediocrity, the former has achieved complete freedom from the dissimulation, pain, and hypocrisy of the world. In the land of the dead, man is finally beyond the critical eye of opinion and has nothing but disdain for the living who are still its victims (*ESW*, p. 71).

The defunct Brás's contempt for his ambitions as a living character is illustrated by the rejection of his former goals. Although the character desired to have children three times during his life—once when he saw Eugênia with her mother, again when Virgília became pregnant, and finally when he contemplated marriage to Nhã-lóló —the dead narrator counts the fact that he didn't leave the legacy of our misery to any creature as his "small balance," the only positive thing in his life.

Despite Brás the narrator's dissociation from the time and aspirations of Brás the character, the former sometimes merges into the latter for ironic effects. Brás the narrator knows that Marcela loves only money but he enters into the time stream of the character in reporting Marcela's declaration of disinterested love. His involvement is reflected technically by the rendering of Marcela's speech in free indirect style (*ESW*, pp. 53-54).

When Brás the character meets the pock-marked Marcela years later, even he realizes the irony of the episode of 1822. In asking himself if her beauty was worth all his sacrifices, he recognizes his ingenuousness at that time. The narrator was well aware of this irony all along but did not choose to reveal it. Thus when it suits his artistic purposes, he merges his time with that of the characters.

More telling in regard to the narrator's imprisonment in time is his comment on the necessity not to lose it. If he is free from human time, why should he be concerned about its loss? (*ESW*, p. 182). In his attitude to the grand passion of his life, the defunct Brás Cubas' memory functions in a manner suspiciously like that of living beings. It conveys pure enjoyment because the painful emotions of the experience remembered are not present (*ESW*, p. 28).

The emotion-proof aspect of Brás's memory is the distinctive feature of his rendering of character time. The great emotional moments of his life are all subject to human egotism, trivia, and the irreversibility of time leading to death. Two such moments are not even evoked through language but are conveyed through rather humorous punctuation marks, the initiation of his affair with Virgília and his failure to become a minister. All that remains of his great passion after twenty years is a limp heart devastated and satiated by life (*ESW*, pp. 28-29). Immediately after his mother's death, Brás admits his own triviality and digresses on an Italian barber, a means of minimizing or nullifying emotion (*ESW*, pp. 70-71). He does the same in relating his father's death and funeral by means of a very short, telegraphic description.[7]

Despite Brás's conscious removal of the dress of emotion from his relived subjective time, he was able as a living character to regain chronometric time through his relations with other people. The first such occurrence is a result of his kissing the young woman who becomes his fiancee, Nhã-lóló. As he came down the hill with the young woman on his arm, he began dropping the years so that at the bottom, he was only twenty years old and had corresponding feelings of gaiety. The second moment is when he is fifty. He becomes younger through the others at the dance and the dazzling atmosphere of the salon, but chronometric time, fifty years, has been registered on his body in contrast to the subjective temporal experience of his mind. The effects of calendar time are inescapable and Brás's years are greedy for sleep and rest (*ESW*, pp. 200-201).

The reader's time is determined by his being drawn into a dialogue with the narrator in *Epitaph of a Small Winner*. The many examples of direct address to the reader, references to specific readers, and digressions all incorporate him into the narrator's time and paradox. We have seen that this time is at least once merged into character time and the reader is enjoined to identify with this time as well: "Well, my ecstasy was like that, friend reader, and if you were ever eighteen you must remember that yours was, too" (*ESW*, p. 52).

Among the specific readers of the work, one of the five the narrator cites in the opening chapter is later addressed as Virgília. To her, he reveals his artistic power to restore the past and judge the content of experience. The vehicle of this power is a book and it is not coincidental that man himself is conceived of as a book. His final edition is definitively corrected by death and given to the worms, symbolic of the cyclical time structure of the planet (*ESW*, p. 77).

The analysis of the three time stacks of narrator, characters, and reader shows that the narrator as one of the creations of the implied author is in control. Although he claims to be outside of time, he is paradoxically caught up in it: witness his fear of losing it. His memory has the same power as that of a living person, but most of all, his manipulation of time reflects artistic concerns. One of these is to show that character time (time of the living) is bound up in human egotism and leads irrevocably to death. Another of these is to engage the reader in his artistic endeavor, to evoke, relive, and make judgments on the past. In a sense, the narrative process itself is the main focus of *Epitaph of a Small Winner.*

"There is no way of constructing a man's life, whether real or fictional, except through reconstructing his past in terms of significant associations supervening upon the objective, historical data, or except through showing the inseparable intermixture of the two dimensions.[8] In the posthumous reconstruction of his life, what are Brás Cubas's significant associations? A careful reading of his narrative shows us that time and its action on human life occupies him most. When a man records his life from a distant time locus, he often has a thesis about it.[9] Because we are dealing with a satire in which the implied author's values are quite distinct from those of his narrator, the latter's thesis is rather difficult to discover. At first, it would appear that Brás Cubas' only thesis is that his life experience was a continuous process of self-gratification. In spite of pleasure derived from this source, he was unhappy and unfulfilled. In his narration, however, I believe that he shows a choice not taken and this is among the significant associations of his life and his real thesis.

The emphasis on time in *Epitaph of a Small Winner* appears early in the work. Chapter VII, "The Delirium," is a temporal allegory in which a hippopotamus transports Brás Cubas to the origin of the centuries. There he meets Nature or Pandora of whom he begs a few more years of life. For Nature, however, time passes with cyclical regularity, inevitably brings death, and continues to subsist under the law of egotism or self-preservation, a prefiguring of Brás's story (*ESW*, pp. 33, 34).

While helplessly watching the passage of the centuries, as regular as a calendar, Brás hopes to see the last one and thus decipher eternity, namely, time and the meaning of existence. As he redoubles his attention, the march of time becomes so rapid it defies comprehension and he emerges from the delirium. Man's passage through time is the repetition of actions and gestures without meaning and his quest to go outside time in order to achieve an atemporal view of life and its significance is contaminated by madness.

In Chapter XLI, the fear of time's action is illustrated by another of Brás Cubas's hallucinations. After his meeting with the pock-marked Marcela, he imagines that the fresh and beautiful Virgília is similarly scarred. Time, which had wrought havoc with Marcela, also destroys Brás's career possibilities which are contingent on the marriage of convenience he is to make with Virgília. The many examples of egotism, avarice, ambition, and hypocrisy all seem to receive their comeuppance from time which, as Nature or Pandora indicates, is utterly indifferent to the less than miniscule concerns of man in the movement of the centuries. Its destructiveness is as natural as the law of preservation. Man's hopes are quickly dashed by the witnessing of time's attrition. Brás Cubas's encounter with Quincas Borba illustrates this. The boy he had known was very different from the man he encountered, indeed separated by an abyss between what he promised to be and what he became (*ESW*, p. 117).

Throughout the Virgília episode, the principal material of the plot, the transiency of human passions is evoked and it is not without reason that time is measured so meticulously—the next day, eight days later, a month later, three weeks later, and so on. Brás's and Virgília's love is compared to an exuberant and fast growing plant of the forest. Brás's analogy of their love to the plant and particularly to the flower is significant in that its duration is brief and limited even though its initial growth is rapid. Virgília's kiss at the gate of her husband's estate was the prologue to the book of their passion and was to end in boredom and satiety. Although he goes away savoring it, Brás Cubas is later keenly aware of the ticking away of his life as he lies awake in bed. Instead of becoming absorbed in the subjective time characteristic of great passions and other emotional experiences, Brás's enslavement to the symbolism of egotism, the irrevocable and destructive passage of clock time, is paramount in his experience. Virgília is one more source of self-gratification rather than a realization of love. He reasons that man will always be subservient to mechanical time and the last one on the earth will look at his watch before he dies (*ESW*, p. 109).

At one point, Brás Cubas compares the emotions of married love to chronometric time. The loss of excitement of early passion brings about a clock-like regularity. Knowing that Brás's conception of time is tied to self-love, this analogy is a very cynical comment on marriage. It seems to form part of man's waiting for death rather than a creative experience (*ESW*, p. 138). Most of all, emotion out of its temporal context is truly anachronistic. Finding an old note of Virgília's, Brás thinks she is asking him to do something outrageous. When he discovers that the note was from a period early in their relationship, he has an odd sensation, particularly since he willingly did what she asked then. This is an example of a text outliving its context and taking on a life of its own apart from the intentions of the author (*ESW*, p. 179).

The most conclusive action of time is death. During Brás's narrative, we witness his own death, his mother's, his father's, Nhã-lóló's, Lobo Neves's, Marcela's, and Quincas Borba's. Whatever else may remain uncertain or unknown, the final end is definite and predictable.

Egotism is the most significant association for Brás Cubas. It is manifested throughout the work particularly in the form of avarice. One character, Viegas, is avaricious even on his deathbed. Cruelty and oppression are a direct result of Brás Cubas's egotism. The description of Quincas Borba's dog fight comes provocatively close to Cotrim's and Sabina's public dissociation from Brás's political journal, indicating their lack of loyalty to him and desire to protect their own interests — survival of the fittest.

If the content of Brás Cubas's reconstructed life was essentially the meaninglessness of an egotistical existence limited by time, what is the narrator's thesis? I believe that the choice not taken, the realization of love in general and in particular, love for Eugênia, would have represented a rejection of egotism and made all the difference in Brás's life. He liked Eugênia, and in her company felt a physical and spiritual satisfaction. Near her, he had a sense of well-being as did she near him (*ESW*, p. 85). Eugênia is more than an actor in a simple eclogue. She is a symbol of love. The "love child" of Dr. Vilaça and D. Eusébia, she is specifically referred to as the goddess of love, Venus. The reservation that Brás's attraction for her was purely physical is countered by his own statement to the effect that he felt moral satisfaction with her. Her lameness ties into the view of human love as imperfect but still the best of all values. Years later when Brás Cubas meets her knowing she has suffered all her life, she is still dignified and forces him to treat her as a lady. It is through this symbolic character that Brás shows his thesis of the choice not taken, one of love made of suffering, dignity, and truth, the only values which give meaning to an existence limited by time.

PHILOSOPHER OR DOG?

The order of *Philosopher or Dog?* generally alludes only indirectly to the specific dates of narrative duration. The year 1869 is the first date given in this manner. In the earliest flashback, Rubião evokes his relationship to Quincas Borba and to the latter's death. We know that this took place in 1869, the year of Brás Cubas's death although the date is not stated in *Philosopher or Dog?* The second date occurs in the same flashback during Rubião conversation with Palha on the train. They speak of the Paraguayan War (1865-1870), another indirect allusion to the year. The third date is a direct reference to a Tuesday of January 1870, and the fourth is again indirect, a mentioning of the German victory in the Franco-Prussian War (1871). The events of the narrative take up three years and it is evident that the omniscient narrator's time is posterior to that of the story.

The straightforward recounting of events is measured in small temporal units. There are approximately twice the number of references to days as there are to hours while months are mentioned least frequently. Unlike *Epitaph of a Small Winner*, *Philosopher or Dog?* relates only three years of a man's life, but they are emotionally charged years and are therefore measured meticulously as in the corresponding periods of Brás Cubas's life. As in the latter's narration, summary, scene and iteration constitute the larger rhythms of the work. Deceleration of time is effected by frequent digressions and flashbacks. Occasional jumps over periods of months cause acceleration while simultaneous space shifts are important in marking the irony shared between narrator and reader as opposed to the ambiguity of the characters. As in *Epitaph of a Small Winner*, these three entities are representative of their own time stacks.

In his time, the omniscient narrator shares ironic distance from the characters with the reader, thus uniting narrator's and reader's time for the most part. Ambiguity among the characters is a result of their egotistical relationships and the mutual misunderstanding of each other's real motives in their time which is plot time. Rubião, a former school teacher from Minas Gerais, inherits the fortune and a grain of madness from the philosopher of *humanitismo*, Quincas Borba. He goes to Rio where he meets Sofia and spends the next three years in a progression from a fantasized adulterous affair with the young woman to delusions of grandeur and insanity until his death, raving.

Early in the narrative, an example of Rubião's misinterpretation of Sofia's motives illustrates narrator-reader distance from character ambiguity. Sofia sends Rubião a basket of strawberries accompanied by a note, which was dictated by her husband as the narrator subsequently informs the reader. Rubião's luncheon guests speculate on the amorous intentions of the sender while Rubião shows his first symptoms of delusion in his fantasy about Sofia's correspondence to his feelings. His fantasy becomes increasingly more elaborate as he seeks secret meanings in a note that she herself had not even composed (*PD*, p. 43).

Rubião becomes more deeply immersed in his delusions during a soiree at Palha's house. While he and Sofia are in the garden, Rubião declares his passion to the young woman and has grasped her hand when they are interrupted by Major Siqueira. Sofia calmly dissimulates by telling the Major that Rubião had just related a joke about a certain Father Mendes. Sofia leaves and Rubião becomes the victim of Siqueira's irony which he is unsure how to interpret. Narrator and reader know that Siqueira had seen the enlaced hands, the inclination of Rubião's head, and the quick movement of both when he came into the garden. Out of all this, astonishingly, came Father Mendes, and Siqueira enjoys and mocks the contradiction (*PD*, p. 54).

In an interconnected network of mutual deception, the characters are each other's victims. Sofia believes Carlos Maria's declaration of love and becomes involved in an adulterous fantasy about him, but he was not sincere. While his motives of the moment were mixed, the underlying one is known in narrator-reader time to be that of unmitigated narcissism. Although he had declared his love to Sofia, it was not true, but to correct his lie would have been worse than the lie itself (*PD*, p. 110).

During one sequence, Chapter LXXXIX to CVI, the narrator's irony is turned against the reader as well as against the character, in this case, Rubião. He imagines that Sofia and Carlos Maria are having an affair. Egged on by a coachman who makes references to a rendezvous on the Rua da Harmonia between a handsome young man with large eyes and a veiled woman and by the knowledge that one of Sofia's dressmakers lives on the Rua da Harmonia, Rubião arrives at the above conclusion when in fact, the narrator tells us that it had no basis outside of circumstantial evidence. He chastises the reader for having gotten into Rubião's time stream and made the same assumption.

Rubião's mental illness, made up of increasing guilt, ambiguity, and delusions terminates in his death. Rubião is in his own time, atemporal insanity, as he crowns himself with nothing while suffering from the delusion that it is Napoleon's imperial crown of heavy gold studded with diamonds and other precious stones. He half utters Quincas Borba's dictum, "to the victor the potatoes," reechoing the central theme of the work, self-love, and survival of the fittest, and dies.

The narrator's final evocation of temporal distance is veiled in chronometric symbolism. In recounting the death of the dog, Quincas Borba, he remarks that the Southern Cross, symbolic of sidereal time, is indifferent to the laughter and tears of men (*PD*, p. 271).

The omniscient narrator's significant associations in recounting three years of Rubião's life resemble those of Brás Cubas in one way and are quite different in others. The prophet of *humanitismo*, Quincas Borba, is present in both works and preaches his philosophy of egotism and survival of the fittest to Rubião who becomes his disciple. Thus, each work gravitates around this central theme but in place of Brás Cubas's insistence on time as the destructive, irrevocable, and indifferent force leading to death, Quincas Borba's narrator evokes the consequences of egotism, madness, and the veritable parade of human vices contributing to this end. If Rubião's initial goals are motivated by self-love, he is a mere lamb among the financial and political wolves of the second reign in Brazil, and a provincial bumpkin among upwardly mobile Rio sophisticates like Sofia. From the outset, the elements of Rubião's madness are present. Thus, he manifests his guilt over the prospect of inheriting Quincas Borba's fortune. He imagines that others will think him responsible for the rapidity of the philosopher's demise (*PD*, pp. 14-15).

Rubião's guilt is not limited to the means by which he becomes a capitalist. His adulterous fantasies about Sofia, wife of Cristiano Palha, cause him equal remorse. Ratiocinating about the scene in the garden during which he had forced his attentions on Sofia,

Rubião is torn between loyalty to Palha and financial considerations and his passion for the latter's wife (*PD*, p. 60).

Ambiguity, another element of Rubião's mental imbalance, characterizes his relationship with Sofia. While she neither encourages or discourages him, she continues to accept his expensive presents, a form of exploitation paralleling that of her husband Palha. As a result Rubião is perplexed when Palha suggests marriage to their cousin Maria Benedita, and weaves a rather tangled web to deceive himself about Sofia's motives. After pondering the match that Sofia is trying to make between her cousin and himself, he concludes that it is simply a subterfuge to throw her husband off the track (*PD*, p. 123).

After various symptoms such as the delusions of grandeur Rubião has about an imaginary wedding (Chapter LXXI), he finally becomes Napoleon III on the one specific date of the narrative, January 1870. Outwardly, he achieves this metamorphosis by shaving himself after the fashion of the French ruler's bust in his study, and inwardly, by ceasing to be Rubião and becoming Emperor of France.

The world around the madman is equally mad along the lines of Quincas Borba's philosophy. The private monomanias are found mostly in the character's views of themselves. Carlos Maria is the supreme narcissist. He thoroughly enjoys the envy and admiration of others. He criticizes Sofia's lack of breeding even if she was the princess of the ball (*PD*, pp. 110-111). Involvement in the human pecking order is another form of madness. The bank director passes on the humiliation he felt at the minister's house to Palha and so restores his own self-esteem. In this chain of deference, each subaltern is subservient to his superior until a new equilibrium is reached (*PD*, p. 135).

Personal vanity comes under the heading of small madnesses and forms part of Rubião's larger derangement. His disinterested act of saving a child's life becomes the subject of a newspaper article. He passes from the shock of first reading the report to appreciating the publicity he had received and its style. He savors the author's repetitions of his name in print (*PD*, p. 96). The world of madness would not be complete without its suspicious-minded inhabitant. Dr. Falcão informs D. Fernanda that he believes Rubião's illness was partially the result of a love affair with Sofia. At first he thinks that D. Fernanda's resistance to the hypothesis is ingenuous but suddenly, his imagination suggests another motive. Perhaps she too had been in love with Rubião (*PD*, p. 233).

Other forms of egotism in this mad world are Palha's avaricious and venal exploitation of Rubião. As the latter enters deeper and deeper into his capital, Palha becomes richer and eventually buys a small palace in Botafogo. In the political arena, Camacho exploits Rubião in a similar fashion. None of these people shows any compassion for the *mineiro* once his madness becomes known, but neither do the people who have been victims of their ambition. Among the first sacrifices of Sofia's social climbing are Major Siqueira and his daughter. As Palha and Sofia move up the social ladder, they cease to invite Siqueira and his daughter since guests with much more social prestige are present. Nevertheless, they have learned nothing from their suffering and are just as cruel to Rubião as the others when he appears at their house hallucinating.

The significant associations of *Philosopher or Dog?* may be interpreted as a vision of madness resulting from the society's value of self-love. While Rubião is the most dramatic example and we follow his life's events, the other inhabitants of this world are also mad but do not become clinically so because unlike Rubião, they have no doubts or guilt. The world of *Philosopher or Dog?*, like that of *Epitaph of a Small Winner*, has satirical elements with the philosophy of Auguste Comte receiving the brunt of the attack with a bit of Darwinism thrown in. Thus, the dog, Quincas Borba, is singled out as the recipient of the only example of disinterested love, that of D. Fernanda who attends to him after Rubião's incarceration. Comte, who spent some years in mental institutions, believed that the dog, the most faithful of man's companions, shared in his spirit. Unlike Brás Cubas's narrative, however, *Philosopher or Dog?* does not manifest the wit implicit in a satirical attack on society. It conveys more of a sense of pathos over the fates of Rubião and the dog as well as an echo of this element in that of D. Tonica, the forty-year-old spinster whose fiance dies shortly before their wedding date. The narrator's final admonition to the reader to cry if he has tears, if not, to laugh because neither action has meaning in the universe seems even more pessimistic than Brás Cubas's small balance but somehow not as effective. The witty prowess of the dead narrator's sarcastic and satirical narrative is a more efficacious chastisement of society's mores than the ironic distance of the omniscient narrator of *Philosopher or Dog?*

DOM CASMURRO

Dom Casmurro, Bento Santiago, begins his narrative with two explicatory chapters, one on the title of the work and the other on his motives for writing it. He then goes back to November 1857 when he was fifteen. His mother, D. Glória, who was then forty-two, had been a widow since 1846 and had destined Bento to the priesthood. When he is little more than seventeen, he leaves the seminary, a goal which various characters worked toward in opposition to Glória's promise to God. He and Capitu are married in 1865 and remain childless for two years. Their friend Escobar dies in 1871 and when their son, Ezekiel, is five or six in 1872, Bento makes his accusation of adultery against Capitu. By the time Ezekiel returns to Rio after his and Capitu's exile to Switzerland in 1872, he is a grown man. One other given date is 1882, marking Bento's meeting with the author of the Panegyric of Santa Mônica, so we know that the narrator's time perspective is from the early to mid 1890s. The narrative ends where it began, in the presence of the solitary and middle-aged Dom Casmurro.

As in the preceding novels, there is a rhythmic alternation among summary, scene, and iteration, but this last element receives more emphasis than in *Epitaph of a Small Winner* or *Philosopher or Dog?* The iterative passages describe the habitual actions of the characters once but the reader understands that these occurred repeatedly. Thus Uncle Cosme's daily mounting of an old nag, the childish games of Bentinho and Capitu, Bento's accumulations of prayer debts to God, his friendship with Escobar, and later his fights with Capitu are a significant part of the larger rhythmic structure. There are approximately the same number of flashbacks as iterative passages which decelerate narrative time. The same effect is achieved by the many digressions which occur twice as frequently as flashbacks and iteration. Two large temporal jumps effect acceleration, one from the years at the seminary to Bento's graduation from law school, and another from 1872 to Ezekiel's manhood. A briefer jump is measured by an indefinite number of months. There are relatively few references to smaller units of time. A series of days, Friday, Saturday, and Sunday, measures Bento's resolution to commit suicide, his viewing of *Othello* and what the play suggests to him, and his consequent projected poisoning of his son, a highly dramatic period. The one reference to the hour is when the adolescent Bento discovers that Capitu has eyes like the tide (*olhos de ressaca*), a central image of the work which is symbolic of the sea of life and the risks of love. The one prolepsis in the narrative is the anticipation of Escobar's death, mentioned before it actually occurs in the sequence of events.

An attempt to analyze the time stacks of narrator, characters, and reader leads to the conclusion that they all merge. Casmurro attempts to recapture time in this novel through affective memory or the reliving of past events.[10] Unlike Brás Cubas, Casmurro is not reluctant to relive the sometimes painful experiences of his life. At one point, he rather masochistically relates that through memory, past suffering becomes pleasurable (*DC*, p. 151). The principal effect of the narrator's complete identification with the emotions of the characters is to bring together their time streams. The reader, creation of the implied author, is also caught up in this stream as a result of being forced to collaborate in the creative process. Consequently, time in *Dom Casmurro* is essentially plot time. In the second chapter, Casmurro tells us that his purpose was to tie together the two ends of his life, to restore adolescence in old age. He did not succeed in putting back together what had been nor what he had been (*DC*, p. 5). He desires to restore subjective time which marked the period of his life before his living death or the death of his emotions. Accordingly, his most specific references to time outline the "plot" of his life—love of Capitu, friendship with Escobar, marriage, projections of guilt over his own adulterous desires, and the jealousy which leads to the destruction of his happiness and family. All of these events are subject to Casmurro's affective memory and are the equivalent of what he calls "*saudade*" (nostalgia), but he defines them in terms of the powers of recollection. For him, longing is the passing and repassing in review of old memories. His memories of kissing Capitu are the sweetest, the most all-embracing, and revealed him to himself (*DC*, p. 72). Only heaven can mark the time Bentinho spends looking at and loving Capitu, an observation which leads the narrator to digress on celestial and infernal time (*DC*, p. 67).

The Panegyric of Santa Mônica causes Bentinho to relive the

years at the seminary. His reference to that time occurs in Chapter LIV and is followed in Chapter LVI by an elaboration of his particular friendship with Escobar (*DC*, p. 109).

The period following Bento's marriage to Capitu is atemporal, so great was their bliss (*DC*, p. 193). The devil's time invades God's time when Bento is attracted by Sancha and contemplates adultery (*DC*, p. 224). His jealousy is short by clock time, intense, and powerful enough to destroy and reconstruct heaven, earth, and all the stars, a configuration of the events of the novel and its artistic implications: "So little time? Yes, so little time, ten minutes. My fits of jealousy were intense, but brief: in an instant I would tear down everything, but in the same instant I would reconstruct the sky, the earth and the stars" (*DC*, p. 202).

The time streams of narrator, characters, and reader flow together through the action of Casmurro's memory and art. Casmurro's many references to time underscore his preoccupation with it, and its effect on his life. Like Brás Cubas, Casmurro witnesses the deaths of all the people around him, Capitu, his mother, cousin Justina, José Dias, Uncle Cosme, Escobar, and Ezekiel. Through his own destructiveness and time's irreversibility, he is left alone with the sole consolation of writing a book and the unsuccessful attempt to tie together the two ends of his life, to restore subjective time.

Among the significant associations of Bento's life, the space he devotes to an evocation of his adolescence is three times as long as that which related the rest of his life. The brevity of the second part may be due to a desire to augment its dramatic quality. Bento of the earlier phase was loving as opposed to Casmurro of the destructive phase, but nevertheless, all the seeds of the latter are in the former and the book's real purpose, to dupe the reader into believing Bento's accusation against Capitu and thus assuage Casmurro's guilt is there for the attentive, involved reader to discover. Bento is predisposed to the idea of being betrayed, particularly by a woman. His own mother had promised him to the priesthood against his will even though she comes to repent of this vow. At one point, he compares her action with Abraham's sacrifice of Isaac (*DC*, p. 157-158). As a result, Bento's doubt and insecurity about people who love him and are close to him becomes exacerbated rather easily and it is predictable that his beloved Capitu and his friend Escobar will be victims of it.

Bento's first episode of jealousy occurs when José Dias tells him that Capitu is happy and doing her best to catch one of the local dandies (*DC*, p. 126). This incident is one of Bento's many evocations of the jealousy which ultimately destroys his life.

The sincerity of Bento's love for his mother is questionable if we consider an instance of one of his innermost feelings and guilt that arises from it. In hopes of getting out of the seminary, he wishes his mother dead (*DC*, p. 136). On the basis of this incident, we may question Bento's love for Capitu. Jealousy is more an aspect of self-love than love for another and consequently the narrator's attempt at catharsis through the telling of his story reflects a great deal of guilt.

Lack of self-esteem or personal inadequacy are closely related to the experiencing of extreme jealousy. Thus Bento's admiration of Escobar's mathematical ability is the first sign of this. Bento's self-doubt increases when he is unable to sire a child like Escobar's and culminates in his recognition of his friend's superior masculinity. This feeling comes over him as he feels Escobar's arms while thinking of Sancha's. He was aware that they were thicker and stronger than his own and that in addition, Escobar could swim (*DC*, p. 223). The final step in the loving Bento's transformation to the destructive Casmurro is his projection of guilt over an adulterous impulse toward Sancha. For him, the pressure of Sancha's hand and his own was a moment of madness and sin (*DC*, p. 223). His subsequent attack of violent jealousy over Capitu's reaction to Escobar's death, the imagined resemblance of his child to his friend, the intention of suicide and murder, and the accusation of adultery with its consequent separation and destruction of his life all follow most logically from Bento's psychology. Bento's jealousy may thus be viewed as another example of the monomanias afflicting many of Machado de Assis's characters.

What is most fascinating in this novel is not the story itself but the artistic process in which the reader is forced to participate in order to penetrate the meaning. The many clues, digressions, and direct addresses to the reader should put him on guard about Bento-Casmurro. If the narrator really wished to convince us of

Capitu's guilt, he would never have revealed as many of his own defects as he did. Thus the significant associations of D. Casmurro, the content of the time he recounts, are more artistic than moral or psychological. The narrative process itself is the main focus of the work. Its importance is attested to by the fact that the reader's response to it is what gives meaning to *Dom Casmurro*.

ESAU & JACOB

The omiscient narrator of *Esau & Jacob* recounts events occurring between the years 1871 and 1893, although the initial flashback reverts to 1855. Up to 1888, time segments are given by year. In 1871, Natividade, mother of the twins, Pedro and Paulo, visits the "Pithia of the North," the *cabocla* Bárbara. In the first flashback, Natividade's pregnancy is announced in August 1869. Santos, her husband, had arrived in Rio in 1855 and married Natividade in 1857. The twins were born on April 7, 1870. The narrative resumes and jumps over seven years to 1878 when the twins were seven. In 1880, they silently witness a servant's theft of a watch, a significantly symbolic action in Machado de Assis's novels relevant to the passage of time. Natividade is now forty. On her forty-first birthday, she receives the title of baroness. There is another jump over five years to 1886 when the fifteen-year-old Flora appears in the narrative. A jump of two years brings us to 1888, the year of emancipation. From this point to the end of the narrative, time is measured in smaller units of hours, days, nights, weeks, and months except for one jump between 1889 and 1891. The daily lives of the characters are projected against the backdrop of the historical political events following emancipation in May 1888. In November 1889, the monarchy's swan song occurs at the ball of the Ilha Fiscal. On November 15, of that year, there is a revolution by the military and November 3 of the following year witnesses Deodoro's dissolution of the national congress. Twenty days later, Deodoro passes the reins of government to Floriano, who reestablishes the congress and annuls the decree of November 3. February 24, 1891, is the date of a new constitution, but political turbulence in national life marks the period following, during which Flora dies. An undetermined number of months later, the twins open professional offices and approximately a year from then, they become deputies. A flashback to the *cabocla* of 1871 who predicted greatness for them is followed by Natividade's death and a symbolic reference to time, the eternal flower in Ayres's buttonhole.

Like the previous Machadean novels examined, *Esau & Jacob*'s larger rhythms lie in the alternation of summary, scene, and iteration. Digressions and flashbacks decelerate time while the jumps cited above accelerate it. Prolepsis occurs rarely and is limited to a reference to information to be given in a later chapter. The narrator is clearly aware of rhythmic problems in his discussion of the temporal discrepancy between writing and reading time as opposed to that actually filled by a speaker (*EJ*, p. 33).

The time of *Esau & Jacob*'s narrator is posterior to that of the characters. From his temporal perspective after the events he recounts, he records the characters' passage through and relationship to objective and subjective time, including its reliving through affective memory. He also evokes Flora's atemporal paradise. His own digressions on time concentrate on its symbolic manifestations. The narrator's instructions and commentary addressed to the reader incorporate the latter into the former's temporal stream if the reader is participating fully and is able to use the glasses given by the narrator in order to decipher intertextual allusions. From this privileged vantage point, narrator and reader view the characters' time in which the past, present, and future intertwine. The inhabitants of the allegorical world of *Esau & Jacob* contemplate and aspire to an ideal symbolized by Flora. Although she dies and the characters do not realize her significance in their lifetimes, flowers of human idealism are eternal and serve as a reminiscence of Flora's atemporal paradise.

Time, then, is the narrator's major preoccupation and he digresses constantly on this subject. For the most part, his reflections are on art, immortality, and the passage of time. The filling up of time can be an infinitely artistic activity as the narrator reminds us in one of his asides on the tempo of the work, in this case, an acceleration. He observes that one can weave anything on the invisible fabric of time but to fill something invisible with nothing is extremely subtle if not impossible (*EJ*, p. 60).

One of the motifs of the narrator's creation, a flower, is symbolic of eternal time. In the following passage, we see the novel's imagery as a microcosm. Flowers continue to bloom and fade regularly despite the beginnings and ends of political regimes. What the flower represents against the backdrop of events from 1888 to 1893 is a note of optimism for mankind (*EJ*, p. 177).

Another of the novel's symbols of eternal time is love and lovers. In a world in which they are dominant, there will be no need for governments and there will be a reversion to the anarchic organization of the first days of paradise. In the following passage, it is significant that the specific person who inspired the digression is a lover of Flora so that the love and floral symbols merge. This is not the last time we read of eternal paradises in connection with them. Because the world belongs to lovers, a day will come when anarchy as in the first days of paradise will prevail. Lovers will be forever (*EJ*, p. 235). The floral and love symbolism of an anarchic paradise becomes more explicit and comprehensible in philosophical terms which are elaborated below. On a day-to-day level, time is a dragon which everybody tries to kill on various occasions. Despite the most vigorous of blows, it dies only to be reborn. Despite deep wounds, the dragon never dies. The three men in question left the dragon stretched out on the ground (*EJ*, p. 219). The narrator warns the reader that the reborn dragon, time, has the potential to destroy the pleasures of youth and advises her not to get into the bad habit of aging. This advice is part of the narrator's concern with and fascination by the passage of time and its effects. The narrator's digressions on time point to the meaning of the allegory and are most pertinent to its deciphering. Time sets the limits of human experience but it is what man contemplates or aspires to which determines his true fulfillment or realization within it.

Plot or character time is an exploration of its own many faceted incarnations. The present is measured in organic time as reflected *ab ovo* from the gestation, birth, and growth of the twins, Pedro and Paulo. They represent the future as well in the *cabocla's* prediction of greatness for them. The older generation with its memories evokes the past so that the society of *Esau & Jacob* reflects three temporal dimensions. Within them is the consciousness of the distinction between subjective or psychological time and chronometric time. The latter measures the days which mark numerical units such as Natividade's fortieth birthday, which in turn has a psychological impact on her. Even though it is only one day later, a question of numbers, she believes herself to be old as of this date (*EJ*, p. 54).

The distinction between chronometric and subjective or psychological time is carefully drawn again in the narrator's evocation of time enjoyed by D. Cláudio, Flora, and Paulo. They spent time in their shopping but there was no record of it since none of them consulted a watch (*EJ*, p. 147).

The reliving of past time through affective memory is a common occurrence in the narrative. In the case of Santos, this reconstruction is not always accurate, but it is typical of human memory which suppresses and adds things in this process. Santos does not always tell the truth because time alters or diminishes things. His memory might have been confused, he might have lost details and invented others. Still, history goes on (*EJ*, p. 59). Memory and its power to recapture past time is a mental activity which is subject to rapid transitions through its associative quality. Ayres has been reliving an interlude with a Spanish actress in Caracas when something in the present interrupts his reverie and changes its focus. Psychological time has the capacity to move in all directions. The story goes forward because Ayres's memory of Carmen and her song disappear upon the appearance of a donkey at the scene (*EJ*, pp. 101-102). Batista, who would sell his soul for political success, would turn back time to correct a strategic error in his career. The march of history is determined by chronometric time, however and in contrast to memory which can manipulate subjective time, Batista is unable to reverse the course of clock time, elsewhere associated with egotism. The future is present from the opening scene of the narrative when the *cabocla* predicts "future things" (*cousas futuras*) for Pedro and Paulo. Throughout the narrative, Natividade projects her hopes for her son's greatness. In looking forward, she borrows the happiness of the future in the event that she might die before the prophecies came true (*EJ*, pp. 120-121). Ayres represents a temporal contradiction. While we have seen his attachment to the past, he desires to kill time, the present, and yet has a great deal of remorse about aging, that is, advancing into the future. This attitude is typical of human nature but in the case of Ayres, it points to his singularity in the society of *Esau & Jacob*. He wanted to apply his senses to a world that could kill time. When he sees Flora's attention diverted to the young men, he regrets growing old (*EJ*, p. 86). Nevertheless, it is his philosophical contemplation which brings him closer to the atemporal ideal Flora represents, symbolized by the eternal flower in his buttonhole which concludes the narrative. In order to understand the full implications of her symbolism, we must turn to the more image-laden passages of the narrative.

If we accept Flora's significance to be that of an ideal of human perfection or fulfillment, she may also be viewed in a Platonic context. Man's quest for perfection aspires through love to the good and the beautiful. Dante's Beatrice with whom Flora is compared in Chapter XCIII (Beatrice for two) is a human embodiment of the divine, a Catholic view which translated back to its Platonic origins is equivalent to the contemplation of the good. The twins, Pedro and Paulo, aspire to peace and justice respectively and are the two who seek in Flora the significance of Beatrice. As Flora plays a sonata, a time during which she transcends her environment, she envisages an atemporal nonspatial paradise not unlike the state of ideal excellence of the Symposium. Government does not exist here and in it are echoes of the lover's paradise cited above. Flora and her vision are man's eternal aspiration to perfection through love in order to achieve the good (*EJ*, pp. 176-177).[11] Flora desires two manifestations of love at the same time, Paulo's desire to change the world and bring about justice and Pedro's wish for stability and peace. The twins become one at the moment of her delirium before death. In a perfect world of love, justice and peace will prevail and in accordance with the Platonic state of having brought forth true goodness, man will become immortal himself.

The combined perspectives of narrator and reader and that of the characters in *Esau & Jacob* reflect a constant and intensive exploration of man's relationship to time. As in Brás Cubas's narrative, the escape from this tyrant is to be found in spiritual values, specifically love. The belief that this ideal could be bought with money is laughable. Flora laughs at the proposal of the nouveau riche Nóbrega. She is equally indifferent to politics and withdraws into an atemporal, pure ideality to escape her parents' conversation. For Flora, music was outside time and space, pure idea. Against the noise of her parents' political machinations, Flora ascends with her music in order to escape men and their dissensions (*EJ*, p. 176).

Keeping in mind the interpretation of the allegory above, let us turn now to the narrator's significant associations. Essentially, the narrator relates twenty-five years of the lives of the twins, Pedro and Paulo, and of the people around them. These particular years focus on the end of the Brazilian Empire and the beginning of the republic. The allegorical format of *Esau & Jacob* is satirical to the extent that its inhabitants are afflicted by a variety of vices such as we have seen in the previous works. These are embodied in very narrow goals and in a larger sense, impede the characters' attaining of fulfillment. Thus, the epigraph from Dante about souls who do not complete their destinies alludes to them. With the epigraph, the characters are rounded out and the reader is given some assistance in penetrating the narrative (*EJ*, p. 41).

More than one-third of the book is devoted to an elaboration of the Santos family, Natividade, her husband, her sister, and especially to the twins, Pedro and Paulo. The remainder of the work describes events which took place in their lives between 1888 and 1893, the years of the transition between the empire and the republic.

Natividade's limitation is in her overweening desire to have her sons realize greatness. Although she witnesses their taking seats as deputies, the fact of their disunity is a constant preoccupation for her which she tries to remedy throughout her life to no avail. Her awareness of their uterine fighting is secondary, however, to her ambitions for the twins. The *cabocla* predicts greatness for them and fighting between them in the world as they did in their mother's womb. Their future glory rests with things fated to be (*EJ*, p. 10). Santos desires status and prestige. Although he is of humble origin, a fact he tries to cover by holding mass for his poor and obscure relative in an out of the way place in order not to be recognized, he covets the most luxurious and opulent status symbol around, the palace of Nova Friburgo, as a fitting monument to his person (*EJ*, p. 32).

The ambitions of D. Cláudia and Batista are purely political. They are compared to Macbeth and Lady Macbeth in their unmitigated and unscrupulous ambitions. They consider and carry out any action that will bring political advancement. Batista's and D. Cláudia's opportunism culminates in his changing parties.

Ayres enters into the allegorical sphere by virtue of his contemplation of Flora and his spiritual fatherhood of the twins. He is apart from the society of petty desires and imagines that if he had been the twins' father, in other words, father of the two impulses toward justice and peace, they would have been unified through the equilibrium of his spirit. From his oblique perspective, Ayres sees through the other satirized characters. He dislikes Santos's materialistic orientation in life and thus further dissociates himself from the values of the society of *Esau & Jacob*. Santos inspired an aversion in Ayres. He didn't wish to harm him but he would have wished him well only if there had been a wall between them. His person, his values, his comments, his laugh, the whole man offended him (*EJ*, p. 128). In like manner, he is able to discern the core of Custódio's dilemma. The sign advertising his pastry shop has political connotations but the many suggestions for making it neutral fail because as Ayres concludes, terror and avarice go together (*EJ*, pp. 161-162).

The theme of avarice is developed more fully in the elaboration of Nóbrega. A former member of a devout society which solicited contributions for masses to be said for the souls of the dead (an *irmão das almas*), he received a donation from Natividade after her visit to the *cabocla*. Because she was very happy, it was a large gift. Nóbrega did not turn it in to the society of *almas* and went on to increase it with many more, specifically during the *encilhamento*, a period of heavy speculation. All of his values emanate from the acquisition and possession of money which he believes will buy anything, even Flora.

The extensive evocation of the political environment of *Esau & Jacob* has led to an interpretation of Flora as a symbol of the ideal republic. The agitation surrounding her death seems to reinforce this idea. This does not necessarily conflict with the significance I have assigned to her, but it would seem to be only a part of it, that part which would eliminate the need for the less noble aspects of politics. Flora's atemporal paradise is anarchic, and the development of its imagery leads me to believe that it is more universal, nonspatial, and atemporal than the narrower interpretation as the ideal republic which failed in Brazil between 1888 and 1893.

In order to arrive at this or other readings of the novel, the reader must participate fully in the narrative process. This is the constant feature of Machado de Assis's most experimental novels, *Epitaph of a Small Winner* and *Dom Casmurro* and it reaches its culminating point in *Esau & Jacob*. It is the narrative technique itself that is the main focus of the novel.[12]

COUNSELOR AYRES' MEMORIAL

Counselor Ayres' Mermorial is a diary covering the dates January 9, 1888, to August 29, 1889. As such, it is meticulously dated according to the entries of its author Ayres, which are chronological but not daily. There are single days as well as groups of three, four, five, or six days with no entry. On occasion, Ayres records his impressions by hour, the smallest temporal unit in the work.

Despite its form, *Counselor Ayres' Memorial* shares certain rhythmic features with the preceding novels. The main activity of a diarist is to summarize, but there are also scenes and iteration contributing to the tempo. As in other novels, time is decelerated by flashbacks which elaborate characters' histories as in the cases of Fidélia and Tristão, and by digressions which may be considered standard for a diary. Accelerations are effected through the jumps over days and periods of days.

The time of the narrator is very close to that of the characters since he records events within a matter of days after they occur. The reader is brought into this stream by virtue of sharing the intimate reflections of Ayres so that for all practical purposes, we are dealing with character or plot time.[13] By the date of the second entry, January 10, 1888, Ayres has characterized himself and his sister, Rita, and has introduced the interest of the work, would the widow Noronha, Fidélia, marry again? By February 10, Ayres has established the network of his social relations and elaborated the characters of Aguiar and Carmo, Fidélia and Tristão. Remaining on the fringes of life and love, Ayres records and speculates on other people's involvements. He interweaves the question of abolition into his diary as a public issue contemporaneous to the particular events in the lives of his characters. Through his social encounters with Fidélia and the people around her, Ayres focuses on her life during the writing of the *Memorial*. He elaborates the quarrel with her father over her choice of a husband, the latter's death, her widowhood, and her close relationship to Carmo. Carmo's other "child," Tristão, arrives in July shortly after the death of Fidélia's father, and his presence causes a resurrection through music in the young woman. Her uncle discovers Fidélia playing and asks her what kind of a resurrection this is? She speaks of the ways of a dead woman but he is pleased with this resurrection (*CAM*, pp. 90-91). By November, Tristão is in love with Fidélia and by January, 1889, his feeling is reciprocated. They are married in May and leave for Europe in July.

In the interim, the historical event of emancipation is overshadowed by private happiness: "There is no public joy that is worth a good private one. I came away just now from *Flamengo* with this thought, and am come to set it down on paper, along with what gave rise to it" (*CAM*, p. 45). The characters, however, are very much involved in the question of abolition. Fidélia inherits a plantation from her father but before her marriage to Tristão, she signs it over to the freedmen. Ayres's comment on this development is very subtle and indicates his awareness of a perennial problem, how to incorporate the dispossessed into a system like capitalism. He ends his commentary in an ellipsis: "There goes Santa-Pia to the freedmen, who will probably receive it with dances and with tears; but it also may be that this new, or first responsibility . . ." (*CAM*, p. 181).

Through his observations of love shared among the other characters, Ayres who initially could not give love, comes to a realization of it. The plot time of *Counselor Ayres' Memorial* is simple and straightforward. The diary is, however, as much a guide to what goes into a work of the imagination as it is a chronological record of a certain period of the narrator's life. Many of the narrator's significant associations are as much about the craft of constructing a story as about the content itself. To recapitulate earlier comments on Ayres's writing preoccupations, he does not write things down immediately after hearing them but waits to write the worthwhile things his memory will retain. He is also concerned with brevity and laments the fact that his writing is not more concise and less sentimental. For idle or retired people, time is in excess especially if one starts to write (*CAM*, pp. 31-32). Other writing preoccupations are with symmetry in a work of the imagination and how to extract novelistic interest from human events.

As for the most significant associations of Ayres's diary, they are constituted by his movement from the fringes of existence to a participation (vicarious though it may be) in love and life. This is first marked by his changing attitude toward Fidélia. He moves from an autumnal attraction to the young widow to an esthetic appreciation and finally to a comprehension of her spiritual qualities (*CAM*, p. 68). Ayres comes to his final realization of love through his observation of the love shared among the old couple, Aguiar and Carmo, and their two fictitious children, Fidélia and Tristão. Life leaves death and old age as the young couple go off on their own to Europe leaving the old couple and Ayres behind.

In its consciousness of literary technique and its content of a realization of spiritual love, *Counselor Ayres' Memorial* is relevant to an understanding of the other novels analyzed. In this work, the reader is exposed to the inner workings of the novelist's craft. As we have seen, this feature is common to many of Machado de Assis's novels, particularly the most experimental of them. *Counselor Ayres' Memorial* differs from the latter in that it is not satirical. There is no distance between the values of the implied author and those his narrator Ayres comes to realize. They both hold love to be the greatest good. In its emphasis on craftsmanship and the value of love, *Counselor Ayres' Memorial* may be viewed as a key to the other novels.

NOTES

1. Riedel, op. cit.

2. For a recent study on time structures, see Genette, op. cit.

3. Georges Poulet, *Studies in Human Time*, trans. Elliott Coleman (Baltimore: The Johns Hopkins Press, 1956), p. 24.

4. Dirce Cortes Riedel points out that Machado de Assis was fully aware of the distinction between chronometric and subjective time and made use of this distinction in his art. Op. cit., p. 30.

5. Harvey, op. cit., p. 111.

6. "It is the interior rhythm of the pseudo-author-character which gives the rhythm of the narrative." Riedel, op. cit., p. 67.

7. "Emotional time didn't register his father's death." Ibid., p. 79.

8. Meyerhoff, op. cit., p. 27.

9. A. A. Mendilow, "The Position of the Present in Fiction," in *The Theory of the Novel*, ed. Philip Stevick (New York:The Free Press, 1967), p. 259.

10. Riedel points out that "like Proust, Assis tries to recapture lost time in *Dom Casmurro* when the narrator changes from actor into spectator of his life. Assis is between the 19th and 20th centuries but does not align himself with the dominant schools. He goes back to the 18th century and resurfaces with an impressionistic technique of the 20th century." Riedel, op. cit., p.48.

11. Ibid., pp. 1034, 1035. Gomes has aptly placed Flora in the context of Schopenhauer's ideas on music but the Platonic interpretation is still valid if we consider that Schopenhauer attempted to reconcile Plato and Kant. Eugenio Gomes, *Machado de Assis* (Rio de Janeiro: Livraria São José, 1958), p. 214.

12. Observing the configuration of time in the narrative structure of three of Machado de Assis's novels, we see that in the second phase of his fiction, he revolutionized narrative technique in Brazil; see Riedel, op. cit., p. 50.

13. Although I have simplified considerably, Riedel isolates three temporal planes in one instance, that of the judge's narrative which Ayres delays recording in order to write down only what is important, Ayres's narrative, and that of the events narrated. Riedel, op. cit., p. 56.

6

IMPRESSIONS OF CHARACTER

WE have seen that the techniques of characterization during Machado de Assis's early period were similar to those generally found in the nineteenth-century novel. There were striking differences, however, from the processes of the naturalist-realist schools. Technically, this implied an absence of the multiple angle view of character, of the accumulation of descriptive details, and of free indirect style such as occur in certain works of Eça de Queiroz. In Machado de Assis's later novels, we find some of these techniques although their presence does not indicate a full acceptance of naturalist processes, as Alfredo Pujol asserts. Pujol views Machado de Assis's gallery of characters as photographs caught in their flagrant reality. Machado de Assis observed the minutest attitudes and the most insignificant gestures. He was a decipherer of souls. His characters' firm and precise drawing rests on the eternal reality of life.[1]

It is clear that if Machado de Assis used some of the processes of naturalism in a particular way, he never associated himself with the school. His autonomous esthetic route led him to parody naturalist processes, particularly in *Epitaph of a Small Winner*. Philosophically, Machado de Assis's ideal character consisted of a morally integrated human being capable of realizing love and of feeling and acting in accordance with this end. In his art, Machado de Assis repeatedly demonstrates the psychological aberrations to this ideal. We witness it in Félix, Brás Cubas, D. Casmurro, and in many minor characters.

In the later novels as in the first four works, the author sketches his character and follows him through events, a process in which the original outline is partially filled in by the reader. It has already been observed that the narrator-reader relationship is crucial to Machado de Assis's techniques of characterization. The earlier narrators' rhetorical questions directed to the reader later evolve into a greater demand for reader collaboration in the narrative process. Through it, the characters come to life and reveal their truths through the conflicts of their emotions and passions.

The great themes of Machado de Assis's masterpieces serve as characterizing agents as well.They are identified with particular personages. That of self-love or egotism is found in many of the works in various forms but is most closely associated with Brás Cubas. The theme of human obsessions leading to madness and destructiveness describes Rubião with his delusions of grandeur and D. Casmurro's monomania of jealousy. Love is of the realm of Capitu, Eugênia, Fernanda, and Ayres of the *Memorial* while the quest for fulfillment or perfection is of Flora's domain. Time is a critical theme in *Epitaph of a Small Winner* and in *Esau & Jacob*. In the former, it is identified with Brás Cubas's egotism and in the latter with the changing of a political and social order. The narrative process itself is the last of the great themes I will mention and is of particular importance in the three most experimental novels, *Epitaph of a Small Winner*, *Dom Casmurro*, and *Esau & Jacob*. Their narrators are all partially characterized by means of this theme.

The story tellers of *Philosopher or Dog?* and *Esau & Jacob* are omniscient and explain motives, describe interior states, make judgments, and digress. Their roles at the moment of their creation were in contrast to the dictates of Flaubert and Henry James whose theories about the disappearance of the narrator I have observed.

The more interesting of Machado de Assis's story tellers are narrator-agents or those who are simultaneously characters in the novels. In their elaboration of themselves and others, there is a utilization of a lifelike process where events and other characters are observed through a convincing human mind.[2] This "convincing human mind" must be taken with a grain of salt, however, when we recall Brás Cubas's consciousness of literary effects. He defines himself as a lover of parody, slightly contemptuous of the reader, and satiric in his intentions.

One of the earliest indications of Cubas's satirical aims is the recounting of his own death and funeral, a parody of the usual way in which novels are begun. Thereafter, he relates his life story chronologically from birth, evoking his upbringing by an overly permissive father and a weak mother. He tells us the significance of these formative years to his adult life. He candidly admits his negative traits and his utter lack of idealism or principles. His effort to systematize human injustice is the object of the satirist, Machado de Assis, skeptical of all systems and laws. Brás developed a taste for contemplating injustice. He minimized and justified it as well as classifying its parts and trying to understand it in a systematized way (*ESW*, pp. 40-41).

His physical characterization at seventeen is a sketch that captures the spirit of the adolescent on the verge of manhood and indicates his moral traits of arrogance and vanity, already instilled in his character. Endowed with down on his upper lip, which he tried to pass off as a mustache, Brás had lively and resolute eyes. He carried himself with arrogance so it was difficult to know if he was a child with manly ways or a man with childish ways (*ESW*, pp. 49-50).

Brás's evocation of his first love affair and his career at the university reveals him to have been irresponsible in his pursuit of self-gratification, lacking in moral fiber, a playboy, and an intellectual mediocrity. Other episodes he chooses to relate compound this image. At a moment of crisis in his affair with Virgília, Brás vacillates between giving her moral support and his own interests. He demands sacrifice and commitment from her while he risks nothing. His reluctance to see her stems from the fear that he will be tempted to share responsibility in the solution. He subsequently invents an equivocal compromise which he views as a mixture of egotism and compassion but he later views the compromise as a fact of his egotism alone (*ESW*, pp. 140-141).

The parody of systems such as *humanitismo* is seen in Brás's self-characterization. He consistently constructs laws to assuage his egotism. After his interlude with Eugênia, he compares its pain, preoccupation, and discomfort to a pair of tight boots which bring enormous relief when removed (*ESW*, p. 88). A similar law is that of the equivalence of windows. When he has done something unprincipled or immoral, he compensates for the action by opening another window of his soul in order to air out his conscience. This is Brás's typical formula for avoiding responsibilty. In this instance, he refers to a single gold coin he found and returned, subsequently receiving much praise for his honesty. Later, he keeps a larger sum of money he finds on the beach (*ESW*, p. 106). After having corrupted D. Plácida by making her an accomplice in his affair with Virgília, he reasons that she would have had a miserable end if she had not compromised her principles for a price. He concludes with another typical law, vice is often the fertilizer of virtue.

Self-parody and the parody of the dominant schools of literature occur throughout the work. I have observed Brás's travesty of both the tradition of romance and naturalism in the image of himself on a steed from the medieval castle which becomes so worn out by romance that finally the naturalists compassionately take its worm-eaten body and place it in their novels. In a parody of romantic sentimentality, he relates the end of his affair with Virgília. In contrast to the suffering of abandoned lovers of the romance tradition who cannot eat, Brás comments fully on the very good lunch he had that day (*ESW*, pp. 181-182). He continues to mock the idealization of romance and the repugnant details of the naturalist tradition in character drawing of others. He does not idealize Virgília's beauty because he claims this is not a romantic novel in which the author ignores freckles and pimples, but she had none (*ESW*, pp. 76-77).

It is possible that in Virgília's physical characterization, Machado de Assis was also parodying naturalist processes such as the emphasis on sensuous traits in the female protagonist. We know from his criticism of *O Primo Basílio* that he deplored this excess. Repeatedly, Brás evokes Virgília's physical attributes in contrast to the rather sparse linear description of other Machadean heroines.

The erotic details of her heavy breathing, shining eyes, and insatiable mouth are discreetly toned down by the art metaphors which describe her in sculptural terms. She was as tranquilly beautiful as a statue (*ESW*, p. 120).

The emphasis on physical traits is again apparent in Brás's evocation of Virgília's bare arms, a feature that constitutes synecdoche in other works, her white bosom, and shining eyes. His viewing of her is accompanied by a lustful fantasy of her undressing, but is still far from the explicitness of certain naturalist descriptions (*ESW*, pp. 122-123).

Each time Brás meets Virgília, he evokes her physical traits, a preoccupation which suggests that the physical is the real level of their relationship. Years after their affair, Brás's reaction to Virgília again focuses on her epidermal beauty as he comments on her dress, shoulders, and age. Even on his deathbed, Brás is most impressed by Virgília's exterior appearance and completes the sequence of physical evocations (*ESW*, p. 29).

Virgília's moral characterization shows her to be a fitting match for Brás Cubas. She is self-centered and unloving as well as hypocritical and vain. She is not sincere about nor does she have a real commitment to her love for Brás. She could not do without the public consideration of marriage and would therefore never think of running away to be with him (*ESW*, p. 127). Brás evokes her vanity, the cause of his jealousy which she enjoyed provoking (*ESW*, p. 139). Through her gestures, she shows how much she cares about nobility. Although she denies it, she wants very much to have a title, a reflection of a bankrupt value system equaled only by Brás's love of glory (*ESW*, p. 168). Their affair itself would appear to be a parody of similar plots in the tradition of romance and naturalism. Unlike the idealized love of the former and sometimes sordid quality of the latter, Brás's and Virgília's is simply the self-gratification of two egotists.

By way of contrast to the techniques of character drawing in *Epitaph of a Small Winner*, those of the omniscient narrator of *Philosopher or Dog?* are much more traditional.[3] If we trace the characterization of Sofia, we find description, narrative analysis, evocation by art metaphors, evocation by others, and self-revelation through a mirror image, thought, fantasy, and dream. Sofia's first appearance in the novel is when she enters the train from Vassouras with her husband, Palha. She is briefly described by age. Her physical evocation is interesting to follow in that like Virgília's, it occurs frequently but it tends toward synecdoche in its emphasis on eyes, arms, and shoulders (*PD*, p. 32).

The next description is quite detailed for Machado de Assis in its mentioning of color, light, the details of matched pearls, and of physical aspects said to be uncovered because Palha enjoyed displaying his wife (*PD*, p. 103). The narrator uses synecdoche in his final description, again focusing on arms and shoulders (*PD*, p. 265). Rubião's evocation also employs synecdoche, stressing arms and shoulders, but his images reveal him to be an execrable poet who says that Sofia's shoulders look like wax (*PD*, p. 5).

Repeatedly, the narrator describes Sofia in terms of art metaphors. At one point he compares her to a piece of sculpture which the artist is in the process of perfecting over a period of time (*PD*, p. 45). At another point, Rubião compares her figure to a spray of leaves rising from a vase with her head as a single magnolia in the center, another example of his lamentable poetry (*PD*, p. 49).

Sofia evokes herself through a mirror image. She is very much her own admirer and narcissistically poses in front of the mirror as she dresses and tries on her latest present from Rubião (*PD*, pp. 162-163). Sofia's moral aspect is drawn through narrative analysis of her social relations. She is the proud possession of her husband who particularly enjoys showing her off. Although unenthusiastic about this display at first, she becomes addicted to the admiration of others (*PD*, p. 46).

Sofia's feelings about Carlos Maria's rejection and subsequent marriage to her cousin are barely dissimulated resentment, again analyzed by the narrator. While she feels slighted that her cousin's letters to her are not so intimate, she does not wish to hear all the descriptive details about Carlos Maria which Fernanda's letter exhibits (*PD*, p. 221). Any compassion Sofia has for Rubião's madness is a reflection of self-love. She pardoned it in him because she believed herself to be its cause (*PD*, p. 220).

The narrator analyzes her social climbing. She has a talent for cutting old ties which are no longer in keeping with her new station in life (*PD*, p. 198). Her former friends comment on these snubs. Major Siqueira goes to the point of testing out Palha's and Sofia's repudiation of old friends by questioning him about his wife's birthday, an event the Siqueiras had always been invited to celebrate previously. Upon questioning Palha about the date, the major does not receive an answer. He knows fully that this slight is a consequence of Palha's social climbing (*PD*, p. 189).

Philosopher or Dog?'s narrator uses several techniques of inner characterization in the drawing of Sofia. Among these is self-revelation through thought. Sofia ruminates her confusion to Palha of Rubião's declaration, the indiscretion of Major Siqueira, and the precautions she must take to avoid scandal. Mentally she goes over the events of the past evening and concludes that she is the object of suspicions. She plans to leave the city because she feels she cannot receive Rubião as she had previously done despite her husband's admonitions (*PD*, pp. 73-74).

The omniscient narrator enters into Sofia's fantasy life as well, another revelation of inner character. Here Rubião has invited her to go to Tijuca on horseback. Even though she refuses, her innermost desire is to accept and she fantasizes about the excursion. She imagines herself an assured horsewoman, not dreamy and poetical, but bold. Upon reaching the top, she listens to Rubião's praise as well as receiving his kiss at the nape of her neck (*PD*, p. 199).

The final technique of inner characterization employed in Sofia's drawing is dream, or rather nightmare. Her subconscious thoughts are about Carlos Maria whose name she is writing on the water from a reclining position on a boat. Carlos Maria appears and speaks lovingly to her as Rubião had done, but in contrast to her negative reception of the latter's words, she enjoys Carlos Maria's. They are next in a carriage engaged in amorous conversation when masked assassins board the vehicle and kill Carlos Maria. The leader then tells Sofia he loves her one hundred thousand times more than the other and kisses her leaving a taste of damp blood. She wakes up horrified. The dream can be analyzed as Sofia's frustrated desires toward Carlos Maria which are avenged by his murder and another man's adulation, but which leaves a taste of blood on her consciousness signifying guilt.

In the drawing of Sofia, the frequent occurrence of description and narrative analysis point to a greater emphasis on telling over showing as opposed to the continuous evocation of the first-person narrator-character of *Epitaph of a Small Winner*. The techniques of *Philosopher or Dog?* reflect a lesser degree of experimentation than its predecessor but in certain aspects of the characterization of the female protagonist, we have encountered devices which recur in the drawing of the symbolic female characters, Eugênia, Capitu, and Flora.

Eugênia, in my view, represents the one example of disinterested love in *Epitaph of a Small Winner*. For the most part, it is Brás Cubas who evokes her but in contrast to the drawing of Virgília, there is no parody. Eugênia is a girl of seventeen, dark, and shy with strangers. Her erect, cold, and silent demeanor is indicative of her great sense of dignity and is the principal trait Brás observes (*ESW*, p. 80). Eugênia's dignity translates itself into a kind of regal superiority when Brás sees her on horseback a little while later. In Brás's further evocations of Eugênia he becomes mythological, referring to her "nymph's head." Rather than insisting on physical features, he describes the simplicity and art of her dress. She is in the simplest dress of white muslin and wears no jewelry (*ESW*, p. 83).

Her moral aspect is no less attractive. She is lucid, simple, and charming but even while evoking these traits, Brás cannot desist from noting less spiritual features and speculating on them. He views her mouth as kissable (*ESW*, p. 83). Brás's observation that Eugênia limps a little leads her to comment in a very direct manner that she was born lame. For Brás, Eugênia's beauty juxtaposed to her lameness is a terrible enigma. If beautiful, why lame? Like other symbolic characters in the writings of Machado de Assis, there is an inexplicable aura surrounding Eugênia. I have submitted that Eugênia's lameness is like love, imperfect but superior to everything else. The Machadean protagonists from Félix to D. Casmurro do not understand love. For Brás, the mystery remains a mystery (*ESW*, p. 84).

Like Capitu, Eugênia is adept at dissembling in a charming way. This is a feature not only of the symbolic characters, but of many of Machado de Assis's female characters such as Sofia of *Philosopher or Dog?* (*ESW*, p. 85).

Through dialogue with Brás (self-evocation and evocation by another), Eugênia reveals herself to be the only truthful character in *Epitaph of a Small Winner*. After their interlude at Tijuca, Brás is leaving to do all the things necessary for his and his father's self-centered goals—make a marriage of convenience in order to become a deputy. Eugênia, the love symbol, paradoxically tells him that he has made the right choice and correctly divines his insincerity (*ESW*, p. 87). Brás evokes Eugênia's suffering, the result of her lameness and love, and asks if her presence was necessary to the century indicating his lack of understanding of love (*ESW*, p. 88).

He is still within his own value system, egotism and avarice, when he encounters Eugênia at the end of the novel. Her dignity is paramount but the way she forces Brás to treat her says more about him than about her. He observes that her dignity obliged him to shake her hand as if she were the wife of a capitalist. She would accept no charity from Brás. He never saw her again nor did he find out more about her. She was still lame and sad in his view (*ESW*, p. 222).

All the elements of Eugênia's characterization, beauty of body and spirit, lameness, dignity, truth, and suffering as well as her mythological epithet as the goddess Venus, lead us to believe that she is the first of Machado de Assis's love symbols. The most famous of these is Capitu. According to Helen Caldwell's analysis, Capitu is love, a force which Bento-Casmurro rejects. It is through his eyes that we see Capitu in a sparse physical evocation. At fourteen, she was tall and had two heavy braids. Dark with large clear eyes, she had a straight nose, delicate mouth, and rounded chin. She dressed poorly, having repaired her old and cheap shoes herself. Physical descriptions are few and unlike those of Virgília, do not dwell on the sensuous. Rather, they introduce her moral development as a woman. She was very womanly and reflected an inner spiritual self (*DC*, p. 161).[4] José Dias evokes Capitu's eyes as those of an oblique and dissimulating gypsy, but he later comments on her competence and beauty (*DC*, p. 191).

Bento is captivated by and often evokes Capitu's eyes (*olhos de ressaca*)—eyes like the tide which draw him in. He is also extremely aware of her beautiful arms and jealous of other people's attention to them. As in the drawing of Sofia, synecdoche is prominent in the the impressionistic sketch of Capitu. A more important point, which has not escaped certain critics, is the interconnecting symbolism of the sea motifs in her evocation.[5] At one point, Bento compares Capitu with a sea nymph, Thetis (*DC*, pp. 68-69). As in the case of Eugênia, the symbolic character is a mythological goddess. Her cosmic force is related to the sea, an image we have seen to represent life and love in *Resurrection*, the danger of shipwreck, disaster, and death for those who cannot love.[6] As Caldwell points out, Capitu's eyes like the tide threaten Bento, who it will be recalled, cannot swim. Love is too great a force for him and like Brás Cubas, he does not understand it and rejects it.

The last symbolic character I will examine is Flora of *Esau & Jacob*. Like Eugênia and Capitu, she is inexplicable according to Ayres. She is also referred to as a goddess and obviously is a symbolic character. I have interpreted her significance as a Platonic embodiment of love and beauty, a Beatrice for two, who represents a human ideal of perfection and fulfillment.[7] It is usually the very personal narrator of *Esau & Jacob* or Ayres who evokes Flora in the novel. Her elaboration is effected through contrast, art metaphor, and an impressionistic outline of her physical presence. The narrator is very much aware of his function of sketching as he suggests the lines of Flora's physical aspect. Possessor of a sweet and thoughtful expression, Flora has an aquiline nose, a half laughing mouth in a slender face, and auburn hair (*EJ*, p. 78).

Unlike the power and status hungry people in her circle, Flora envies the Empress only because she has the power to dismiss everybody around her and to remain alone for contemplation or music, a desire which suggests Flora's philosophical implications (*EJ*, p. 122). She is the spirit of justice in her defense of both twins, Pedro and Paulo, a quality evoked by the narrator and revealed by her through speech. Flora's is a spirit of conciliation or justice (*EJ*, p. 215). Flora's spirituality and philosophical connotations make her the most ethereal of the Machadean symbolic characters, but she shares with the other two in the sparse details of her physical elaboration, her enigmatic quality, and her beauty.

Let us turn now to some of the general characterizing techniques of the Brazilian master. The five later novels reflect a predominance of showing over telling, a result of the narrative point of view. Three of those works are recounted by narrator-agents and consequently, a character evokes all other characters as well as himself (showing). In the two novels recounted by omniscient narrators, there is a distribution of showing and telling. Summary including narrative analysis and description is quite frequent in these works. *Philosopher or Dog?*'s narrator gives us a slight physical description of Rubião. He is about forty-one and clean-shaven (*PD*, p. 5).

The seeds of Rubião's mental disintegration are present in his moral characterization in which the narrator analyzes his mental processes. His desire is divided between staying in the small place where he had been an obscure nobody in contrast to his present wealth and going to the glamorous capital, Rio de Janeiro. What he does not realize is that the values of the brilliant life will afflict him with madness and destruction (*PH*, pp. 22-23). It is again the narrator who analyzes Rubião's guilt feelings over Quincas Borba's legacy and the knowledge that the philosopher was mad when he willed it (*PD*, p. 18).

As the story progresses and Rubião becomes increasingly more immersed in his delusions of grandeur and madness, it becomes clear that Machado de Assis chose the process of omniscient narrator for the sake of coherence. By distancing the teller of the story from the protagonist, he was able to control the narrative thread at all times.

Esau & Jacob's narrator is again omniscient even though we know that Ayres, a character in the novel, was its author. The narrator devotes several paragraphs to a description of Ayres's physical appearance and to an analysis of his moral stance. This is in preparation for his somewhat allegorical role in the novel, that of philosophical contemplation. He is outside the circle of petty vices, typical of many of *Esau & Jacob*'s characters, and is a spiritual father to the twins, allegorically, the impulses toward justice and peace. He is also the admirer and contemplator of Flora, whom I have suggested is a Platonic ideal of love. Thus I feel that certain critics have misunderstood Ayres.[8] His initial elaboration is a positive one and is effected by telling: he was forty or forty-two and a fine man. He was a career diplomat on leave from the Pacific. He was a diplomat through and through. His mustache gave him an air of youthful vigor. In his buttonhole, he always wore a flower (*EJ*, pp. 37-38).

In both *Philosopher or Dog?* and *Esau & Jacob* there are also examples of scene or showing in character drawing. Palha, in conversation with his wife, sees Rubião as a yokel and a fool because of his declaration of love to Sofia (*PD*, pp. 69-70). Rubião's servant alludes to his master's madness to amuse his cohorts in the neighborhood. He comments on his grandiose delusional system (*PD*, p. 249).

Flora of *Esau & Jacob* evokes both Paulo and Pedro in thought and imagination, an interior narrative process which reverts to the character (showing). She contemplates Paulo's radicalism which will overturn the world in order to establish justice. Paulo was adventurous and he wanted to remake the world for another purer happier one. He was a perfectionist and she imagined he would be a good husband (*EJ*, pp. 206-207). At the same time, she appreciates Pedro's love of peace, order, and harmony as the desirable qualities in a prospective husband. Pedro was peaceful. He was content with the world and appealed to Flora's idea of perpetual bliss (*EJ*, p. 208). Flora desires both and dies without choosing, a symbolic configuration illustrating man's failure to achieve the two ideals at that moment in history.

In contrast to the human idealism of *Esau & Jacob*, Brás Cubas generally evokes human selfishness. He ironically narrates his father's vanity on the latter's deathbed, gratified by the visit of a minister (*ESW*, p. 97). Another example of the narrator-agents' function of showing is when Bento of *Dom Casmurro* evokes José Dias's astonishment, as reflected by his facial expression after the boy's declaration that he is counting on the charlatan to save him from the seminary (*DC*, p. 52).

Ayres of the *Memorial* evokes the other characters by means of biographical summary and a physical description through which moral elements may be perceived. This is his formula for Fidélia, Carmo, Aguiar and Tristão. The portrait of Carmo is generally believed to be that of Carolina, Machado de Assis's wife, and critics have analyzed her biographical elaboration in relation to the known facts. Whatever the correspondence may be, the work itself is an eloquent and beautiful statement about love in a marital relationship. Although the plot revolves around the question of whether the widow Fidélia will marry again, the very positive and autobiographical view of married love is centered on the Aguiar couple shown by Ayres. He first speaks of their unity. Throughout the years, the two people had become one and single (*CAM*, p. 18). The slight physical descriptions of Aguiar and Carmo reflect their cordiality and warmth. Aguiar all but hugs Ayres and his hand shake is warm and eager. His wife is sweet and charming and her facial expression radiant (*CAM*, p. 18).

One of the most important means of characterization in the works of Machado de Assis is speech, another means of showing. As Maria Nazaré Lins Soares observes:

> Language is one of the means the novelist possesses to characterize his personages. In many writers, it assumes as great importance as other means (description, analyses, flashbacks, etc.) and in Machado de Assis we can say that it is perhaps the most important of the instruments the writer mobilizes to this end. The mediocre personage who naturally does not recognize his own mediocrity as long as certain favorable conditions are present often attempts to climb to a position, attain a prestige which are incompatible with the little intelligence, sensitivity and inventive capability he possesses.[9]

Brás Cubas's father is typically mediocre but reveals his grandiose ambitions for his son through his speech. Rather than encouraging the development of inner strength, old Cubas advises his son that his value will be confirmed through other men's opinions, never taking into consideration their possible and probable mediocrity. He admonishes Brás not to remain obscure and unhappy. The son must live up to the Cubas name and make it more illustrious. In short, Brás must do something with his privilege (*ESW*, p. 78).

Philosopher or Dog? is particularly rich in examples of idiosyncrasies revealed by speech. These are effective in the characterization of mental health, personality, and professional aspirations. The philosopher, Quincas Borba, reveals his doctrine in conversation with Rubião. The madness of his message is immediately apparent, but within it is a satirical criticism of contemporary views on society's acting out of the Darwinian concept of the survival of the fittest. In an amusing passage, he explains the death of his grandmother, run down by a carriage, as being necessary to satisfy Humanity's hunger. After all, Humanity must eat (*PD*, p. 10).

Rubião, Quincas Borba's disciple, inherits not only his master's fortune but his insanity as well. His predisposition to madness is marked by guilt and ambiguity but his other directedness or lack of a strong sense of self is also evident in his drawing. A verbal expression of this trait is his habitual use of proverbs as a means of justifying events in his life. Here, he speculates on his good fortune in having inherited from Quincas Borba instead of the money going to a child who might have existed if his sister had married the philosopher: "See how God writes straight on crooked lines" (*PD*, p. 3). Next, he remembers that all his own enterprises have failed and continues to be amazed at his inheritance even though it stipulates various idiosyncratic demands in relation to the dog, Quincas Borba: "He whom God helps is better off than he who rises early" (*PD*, p. 22). When he is definitely mad, his speech reflects his delusions of grandeur as Napoleon III. He declares his imperial love to Sofia, urging her to call him Louis and addressing her as his sweet, heart's desire (*PD*, p. 215).

Among the minor characters of *Philosopher or Dog?*, there is one who is caricatured on the basis of his speech, Major Siqueira. A classic bore, he talks incessantly, inevitably repeats himself, and tells anecdotes about people and events of no interest to his audience (*PD*, p. 44).

Political rhetoric conveys a humorous characterization of a would-be politician who never makes the grade. At one point, he is called an old maid of politics. The absurdity of his rhetoric is patent as he discusses one of its fine points with Rubião:

"Vile vendors? There's only one thing wrong," said Camacho. "It's the repetition of the v's. Vile ven—vile vendors. Don't you hear that the sound is disagreeable?"

"But before that there's *vés vis*—"

"*Vae victis*. But that's a Latin phrase. We can put something else: vile merchants."

"Vile merchants is good."

"Though merchants isn't as forceful as vendors."

"Then why don't you leave vendors? Vile vendors is strong; no one notices the sound. I never pay any attention to that. I like forcefulness. Vile vendors."

"Vile vendors, vile vendors," Camacho repeated in an undertone. "It's beginning to sound better to me already. Vile vendors. I'll accept it," he concluded. [*PD*, p. 159]

In *Dom Casmurro*, José Dias who is drawn as a charlatan, a hanger-on, and an opportunist, is known for his sonorous and pompous phrases which are marked by frequent use of the superlative. He comments on the sense of duty which impelled him to remind D. Glória of her promise to place Bento in the seminary, in reality, an aspect of his gratuitous interfering in other peoples affairs (*DC*, p. 9).

Closely related to speech as a technique of characterization is the use of gesture. Carlos Maria of *Philosopher or Dog?* shows his repugnance for the dog with a gesture of withdrawal. When the dog tries to lick his hand, he withdraws in repugnance and Rubião kicks the dog causing it to yelp and run off (*PD*, p. 42). Carlos Maria's gestures toward Sofia are no less contemptuous. After declaring his love for the young woman, a lie, he wears an expression of mockery on his face as he dissembles for public consumption. He disguises his feelings from the others. His expression bears the trace of a caustic laugh (*PD*, p. 104).

While gestures and facial expressions often reveal inner attitudes and feelings, there are a number of conventional techniques that convey interior states. Rubião's monologues are usually on the subject of Sofia, and convey his fantasies and desires toward the young woman. He entertains a full-blown fantasy about how much Sofia likes him (*PD*, p. 34). On one occasion, Rubião's thoughts are rendered in free indirect style, a process by which the narrator keeps control but allows the character some autonony thus creating a convincing representation of what is passing through his mind (*PD*, pp. 66-67).

Other techniques of inner characterization are dream and delirium. By means of both, the character's subconscious is revealed. As I have shown, Brás Cubas's delirium is a temporal allegory in which the protagonist tries to fathom the meaning of an egotistical existence but his life is only a minute in the advance of the centuries and the repetition of the human drama. The mother of all men is Pandora or Nature who denies Brás a few moments more of life. She announces that she carries in her box all the good and evil of the world, the greatest of which is hope. As Brás is on the verge of deciphering the enigma of the centuries, he comes out of his delirium. Because of its allegorical and satirical intent, this delving into the subconscious does not function strictly as a technique of characterization except to emphasize the narrator's wit and parody of literary conventions. He declares that as far as he knows, nobody has ever yet related his own delirium. He advises readers who are not interested in psychological phenomena to skip the chapter (*ESW*, p. 30).

In *Dom Casmurro*, dream reveals Bento's subconscious, in which fears and desires are mixed in an elusive way. What seems clear are the elements of Bento's jealousy of and love for Capitu, his view of the lottery as a symbol of hope which may bring the grand prize, happiness, and fulfillment, but which Pádua did not win despite the beautiful symmetry of his number. Bento sees Capitu at the window talking to a suitor and goes up to the window to find Capitu standing next to her father. The suitor had brought the prize-winning list of the lottery and his ticket had come out a blank. He had a marvelously symmetrical number, 4004, and was incredulous that it had not won the grand prize. While Capitu's father speaks of the ticket, Bento receives all the gifts of Capitu's eyes (*DC*, p. 128).

The full implications of the dream are not clear, but Pádua's failure could be read as a prefiguration of Bento's failure in relation to Capitu, if we accept the Freudian view of the importance of a woman's father in her choice of a husband and Bento's equating of lottery prizes with conjugal happiness, which he also does in the case of his parents. As in the delirium, the dream seems more symbolic in its intentions than mimetic, and therefore, functions as a device of characterization only in an oblique way.

One of Machado de Assis's preferred devices of character drawing is the contrast of his people. In *Resurrection*, he declared it to be the interest of the story and we see this pattern not only in his great work, *Dom Casmurro*, but throughout the elaboration of many of his characters. After presenting Freitas in *Philosopher or Dog?*, he asks us if we want to see his opposite. If Freitas is frank and unrestrained, Carlos Maria is affected in his manner and behaves in a cold and superior way (*PD*, pp. 38-39). In the same novel, the contrast to the beautiful Sofia is the sad old maid, D. Tonica. She was thirty-nine and still on the lookout for a partner on whom she could still turn the few sparks in her eyes (*PD*, pp. 47-48).

The contrast between Bento and Capitu is apparent throughout the narration as well as constituting the basis of *Dom Casmurro*'s interest. Capitu's greater commitment to the realization of their love is illustrated by the scene following Bento's revelation that he must enter the seminary. Bento is unconcerned enough to buy sweets and to eat them while Capitu remains reflective (*DC*, p. 39).

Their respective self-domination is another point of contrast. During a scene in which Bento tries to kiss Capitu, they are first interrupted by her mother and later by her father. Capitu is not intimidated by either one of her parents. She is always sure of herself and in control even when interacting with adults, while Bento's tongue becomes tied. His lack of a sense of self is fundamental to self-doubt and consequently, he doubts those close to him.

In *Esau & Jacob*, the twins Pedro and Paulo are contrasted on the basis of their divergent political opinions, and Flora is very different from her parents. The narrator comments that Flora and her parents are almost contradictions of one another. He concludes that children do not always reproduce their parents (*EJ*, p. 73).

Another of Machado de Assis's preferred devices is characterization by means of literary allusion. At one point Brás Cubas compares Marcela's laugh to that of a creature born of a Shakespearean witch and a Klopstockian angel. In *Esau & Jacob*, Batista's political ambitions are compared to Macbeth's. The witches this time are *Cariocas*, who resemble their Scottish sisters. They greet Baptista and prophesy political advancement for him.

The literary epithets for the twins, Pedro and Paulo, are Homeric. Paulo is the angry son of Peleus and Pedro is the crafty Odysseus. In *Counselor Ayres' Memorial*, Carmo is characterized by her love for and keen critical sense of literature. The group discusses French novels at a gathering. Carmo knows more than Ayres or her husband. She summarizes for him and his excellent memory helps him retain what she has told him. Carmo's analysis is more lively and interesting. It is clear to Ayres that if Carmo's husband were a writer, she would think him the best, because she loves him as much or more than on the first day (*CAM*, p. 106). Since Carmo was modeled on Machado de Assis's wife, Carolina, her attitude toward her husband's craft and skill may be viewed as not only one of admiration but as extremely supportive as well.

As in the earlier novels, zoomorphic epithets describe human traits. Brás Cubas compared himself to a peacock and Lobo Neves to an eagle in Virgília's choice of a husband (*ESW*, p. 96). Sofia in *Philosopher or Dog?* is surprised at Rubião's transformation from a dove to a falcon (*PD*, p. 51). The contrast to giving humans zoo-morphic attributes is giving an animal anthropomorphic traits. Not only does the dog Quincas Borba have a man's name, he has singularly human thought processes and is one of the two characters in the novel to understand love (*PD*, p. 34-35).

In *Dom Casmurro*, characterization by photograph occurs three times, once in the evocation of Bento's father and mother and twice in the evocation of Escobar. The photograph of Bento's father and mother seems straightforward enough and convinces him of their happiness which he compares to the grand prize in a lottery (*DC*, pp. 15-16). In like manner, the first mentioning of Escobar's photograph is made without other implications except to evoke his distinction (*DC*, p. 226).

The crucial moment in the viewing of Escobar's portrait is after Bento has accused Çapitu of adultery with his best friend. They look from Ezekiel to the picture and for Bento, Capitu's reaction is the conclusive proof of her guilt. Bento believes that Capitu is guilty when they both look from Ezekiel to Escobar's picture. Bento interprets Capitu's confusion as pure confession. Ezekiel and the picture are one. But Capitu confesses nothing and goes off to mass with her son (*DC*, p. 250).

In psychoanalytical terms, it is interesting to speculate on what we might view as Bento's Oedipus complex. He is outside the happiness represented in the photograph of his parents. His mother's rejection of him is not only a reversal of Jocasta's role but a betrayal, her promise to God that he would enter the seminary. The configuration repeats itself with Capitu and Escobar with Bento still acting out his Oedipal role. The characterization by photograph can thus be viewed as a very suggestive device.

Characterization by letter reveals Quincas Borba's madness. He has discovered that he is Saint Augustine and draws parallels between the Saint's life and his own, with the exception that Augustine thought that evil was a detour of will (*PD*, p. 17). In *Counselor Ayres' Memorial*, Fidélia's letter among other aspects causes Ayres to evoke her spirituality. He calls her letter a genuine page of her soul. Ayres found the letter really interesting and free of convention or high-flown phrases (*CAM*, p. 67).

A review of Machado de Assis's techniques of character drawing shows that he was entirely familiar with those common to his time. In his parody of the dominant schools, he demonstrated autonomy and inventiveness. In his original application of traditional techniques, he was able to penetrate the psyches of his characters from the inside out.[10] His view of life is channeled through his most memorable characters, Brás Cubas, Capitu, Casmurro, and convey Machado de Assis's views on the nature of man.

NOTES

1. Alfredo Pujol, *Machado de Assis*, 2nd ed. (Rio de Janeiro: Livraria José Olympio, 1934), p. 100.

2. Henry James as quoted by Booth, op. cit., p. 45.

3. Despite what appears on the surface to be a reproduction of more conventional nineteenth-century techniques, *Philosopher or Dog?* has been analyzed as a parody of the traditions of romance and realism. Ivan Monteiro and Hairton Estrella, *Metalinguagem em "Quincas Borba" de Machado de Assis* (Rio de Janeiro: Livraria Academica, 1973), pp. 40-43.

4. One must confess what a disillusion [it is] for the admirers of the brilliant, the beautiful, the sensational; if one compares the presentation of Capitu with the descriptions of Alencar in a *Profile of Woman*, the latter's minute descriptions . . . overload the model with a quantity of details, lingering on the curve of the eyebrows, of the lashes, of the mouth, place infinitude in the eyes, an ardent palpitation of life in all the forms and spend a fortune in teeth of pearls and lips of coral. There is a linear dryness on Machadean description, made of one stroke. It is a fasting from metaphors. A more than discreet use of adjectives, it is almost primitive in its simplicity. [Meyer, op. cit., p. 143]

5. Caldwell, *Brazilian Othello of Machado de Assis*.

6. "Of his feminine types, all attractive, products of his suppressed artist's sensuality, she is the most seductive and mysterious. She is full of fatality like the cosmic forces. She is really a cosmic force." Matos, op. cit., p. 235.

7. "One way or another, whether she is called love or piety, hope or glory, Flora centralizes the Platonic transcendentalism which leads to a vision of beatitude like Beatrice." Gomes, op. cit., p. 204.

8. Ayres's attitude toward men, toward events, in the midst of the discussions that take place, is a copy of Pontius Pilate at the judgment of Christ. He always washes his hands as if the problem of

irresponsibility in life could be a decision, as if not acting or not having an opinion could define a personality. If he did exist, he would be eliminated as abhorrent since he wouldn't take account either of the interests of his fellow human beings or of their daily passions. He would be thrown aside like a dry leaf, just as the current of overflowing rivers leaves lightweight bodies on the shores. He has no weight, no center of gravity. [Matos, op. cit., p. 258]

9. Soares, op. cit., p. 24.

10. Meyer, op. cit., p. 147. For an interesting discussion of the techniques of interior realism and characterization, see Moisés, op. cit., pp. 27-28. Also, see João Pacheco, *O Realismo* (1870-1900) (São Paulo: Editora Cultrix, 1963), p. 36, for a discussion of Machado de Assis's characters in their intimacy.

7

A THEORY OF
CHARACTER

MY study of the processes of characterization has aimed at establishing a theory of character in the novels of Machado de Assis. To arrive at a concluding statement, I will examine the meaning of these processes, place Machado de Assis's achievement in the scheme of Harvey's constitutive categories, and apply these findings to what I believe to be Machado de Assis's theory of character.

All of Machado de Assis's narrators are dramatized to the extent that they refer to themselves as "I." There is a division to be observed when these first-person narrators become protagonists, however. Then, all of the techniques of characterization become dramatized, "showing" as opposed to "telling," because a character is evoking himself or others. The novels of omniscient points of view reflect a more gradual increase of "showing" over "telling." In *Resurrection*, "telling" predominates, with extensive use of narrative analysis and description including gesture and animal metaphor. An interior technique (showing) occurs in the use of silent monologue. Speech and evocation by others are also present (showing). In the following novel, the *Hand and the Glove*, there is a better balance between "showing" and "telling" with the addition of metonymy, art metaphors, and characterization through literature. Greater stress on the relations among characters in the next two novels, *Helena* and *Iáiá Garcia*, gives rise to extensive occurrence of "showing" techniques with that of dream introduced into the latter novel.

Philosopher or Dog? utilizes all the methods of the naturalist novel, multiple angle view of character by the narrator, other characters, and the character himself, accumulation of detail, and free indirect style. The interior techniques of showing take the form of mirrored reflections, thought, fantasy, dream, and monologue. Speech is of course another important means of showing character. The techniques of "telling" are narrative analysis and description including gesture, synecdoche, literary allusion, and zoomorphic and anthropomorphíc metaphor. *Philosopher or Dog?*, the most conventional of Machado de Assis's later works, illustrates that he was thoroughly at ease in manipulating these techniques which so resemble the processes of the naturalists but he chose not to do so again. The double narrative effect produced by Ayres-narrator and Ayres-character in *Esau & Jacob* makes it more like the narrator-protagonist novels of Machado de Assis's later period than the omniscient works.

In the narrator-protagonist novels, techniques that occurred in the earlier phase and in *Philosopher or Dog?* appear but are implicitly dramatized. One of these effects is the use of synecdoche. Sparse physical elaboration occurs in the creation of the symbolic love characters whose beauty and enigma are suggested impressionistically. Parody is used in drawing characters who mock both the traditions of romance and naturalism and the philosophical system encompassing the latter, positivism, with its belief in the victory of altruism over egotism. The role of the narrator-character reflects the psychological aspect of the confessional novel in time and makes use of delirium, evocation by letter, literary allusion, and even photographs. Finally, the contrast of "people" serves as a fundamental device particularly in Machado de Assis's best-known novel, *Dom Casmurro*, as well as in its precursor, *Resurrection*. The predominance of "showing" over "telling" lends to Machado de Assis's art a dramatic quality, which he emphasized throughout with his many references to theater and opera, particularly to the works of Shakespeare. On this basis I submit that his later novels in particular have a technical link with great drama.[1]

Let us turn our attention now to Machado de Assis's concern for portraying the reality of esthetic truth. For this, I refer back to Harvey's constitutive categories, time and identity, freedom and causality. A truthful handling of these categories establishes mimetic adequacy, in Harvey's view.

We have seen that Machado de Assis's emphasis on the thematic importance of time marks his art as distinctly modern. He explored the element in its objective and subjective manifestations, in its relationship to the free play of memory, its tyranny over existence, its cyclical repetition, its intensity in emotional periods of life, its maneuverability by psychological processes as opposed to historical criteria, and human fulfillment within it. If anything, Machado de Assis explored this theme and portrayed it much more fully than Harvey was able to in his theoretical descriptions. The critic does make some observations that coincide with the artist's practices.

> We are aware of the richness and freedom of our subjective experience, liberated from time by memory and imagination; yet we are also aware in some sense, of this freedom as contained in an objective organic time, which manifests itself in the larger rhythms of life and nature and which bears us irreversibly in one direction towards one final end.[2]

This statement could be a guide to the handling of time in Machado de Assis's most experimental novels, *Epitaph of a Small Winner*, *Dom Casmurro*, and *Esau & Jacob*. I have shown the exploration of temporal phenomena in these works and that Machado de Assis's management of the dimensions of time is strikingly effective in establishing his character's reality. His insistence on the reader's obligation to participate in this process is evident throughout.

Machado de Assis is fully aware of its temporal aspect when he answers the question of identity, or what is man? His protagonists' quest for meaning is effected through an attempt to relive past time through affective memory. Machado de Assis's concern with the moral natures of his characters is reflected in consistently showing their manifestation of the psychological aberration that impedes unity or fulfillment. The isolation and alienation of his characters may be viewed as another feature of his modernity. What Harvey calls "a sense of duality between Self and World" is mirrored in Machado de Assis's counterpoising of his egocentric characters with their symbolic foils representing love, a possibility for fulfillment which they systematically reject. Harvey comments at length on this process, which provides a theoretical framework for Machado de Assis's art. Harvey calls the process by which one's sense of duality between Self and World is diminished and in which discrete identities form a unified and larger spiritual continuum "psychic decomposition." He explains that this indicates an artistic vision of the world as it splits into various attributes forming different characters. Characters thus exist not only in the context of normal human relations but unite in their single reference to an imaginative vision that "still envelops their individual outlines."[3]

This "single imaginative vision" plays an important role in formulating my theory of character. In the novels of Machado de Assis, the potential for unity in psychic decomposition contributes, in Harvey's words, to "a sense of human life, a dimension of reality, without which we should all be impoverished."[4]

Machado de Assis explicitly commented on freedom in his final novel, *Counselor Ayres' Memorial.* He was concerned with what he viewed as too many symmetries in his diary if he were writing a work of the imagination. He concluded that we are both determined and free and our normal routines dictate a certain amount of repetition which leads to determinism. What interested both Machado de Assis and Harvey was the possibility of the characters' choices within their limited freedom. Harvey states: "The mimetic adequacy of any novel will therefore depend on the novelist's ability to create the sense of man as simultaneously both agent and patient, free and not free, capable of choice yet limited in innumerable ways."[5] Machado de Assis conceived all his characters with the duality between Self and World in mind and the choices this involves. Before their destinies are finalized, they perceive of themselves as free to aspire to their goals even while the reader is aware when they make a fatally wrong choice in pursuing them. According to Harvey, if the conditional freedom that exists between World (limitation from outside) and Self (greater freedom than occurs in life) is not balanced, our sense of mimetic adequacy is strained.[6] If we consider Brás Cubas's life, we are immediately struck by the social and familial restrictions which seem to determine his existence, but as Harvey observes, social mores are often paradoxically a condition of our freedom since they allow us certain advantages we might not have had otherwise, witness the educational, marital, and career possibilities accompanying Brás's social and familial status.[7] Brás's freedom of Self exists but never inspires him to make the right choices. Thus, there is equilibrium in the representation of conditional freedom between Self and World in this work. Machado de Assis's treatment of the category of freedom may have involved a conscious rejection of the naturalistic straining of the equipoise between Self and World based on a determinism made up of heredity and environment. Ultimately, his artistry was the essential quantity in his handling of freedom.

Machado de Assis's interest in causality is, like freedom, related to his discussion of symmetry in *Counselor Ayres' Memorial*. For him, symmetry, or the coincidences of imaginative literature, constitutes a process which imitates life. Both he and Harvey believe that "coincidence expresses a truth about the real world. It expresses our sense that real life blends the casual and the causal, that things are connected and contingent, patterned and random, that we are both free and determined."[8] Causality in the novels of Machado de Assis is closely bound up with conditional freedom and the choices it allows. D. Casmurro's psychological makeup determines his tragic end, but along the way there were innumerable small choices leading to the larger one to reject love. In this sense, he was free and determined. In all of Machado de Assis's characters' lives, there is a play between determinism and choice which inevitably results in failure, except in the case of Ayres in *Counselor Ayres' Memorial*. His awakening came when he had reached an advanced age and illustrates one character's realization of love and his awareness of the choices to be made in attaining it. While Machado de Assis's works have long been thought to reflect a pessimistic view of man, the potential and the example for change are present in the corpus and reflect what I believe to be a somewhat optimistic vision. In my opinion, the representation of time, identity, freedom and causality in Machado de Assis's fiction more than satisfies Harvey's criteria for mimetic adequacy and more importantly, fulfills the artist's aim of achieving a reality based on esthetic truth.

In conclusion, I believe that Machado de Assis's theory of character is metaliterary—based on the values of world literature, a response to the literatures of his time, and conscious of itself as literature. I submit that Machado de Assis's concept of character was partially inspired by Shakespeare and I have observed the dramatic quality of Machado de Assis's processes. If characterizations are equivalent to structures determined by such cultural generalizations as might have surrounded any given dramatic artist in the history of world literature, let us look at those which influenced Shakespeare:

> The essential notion for Renaissance concepts of "order" was love. This notion made obedience equivalent to love in the maintaining of God's ideal order. Man's emotions existed to realize love, his basic drive. If this drive was toward a transcendental rendezvous defined by society as the Good, the Beautiful, or God, personality theory in the Renaissance was asserting a concept of optimum emotion, one to be arrived at by obedience to certain cultural tenets. Freedom was to be gained through obedience.[9]

For Shakespeare, it was commonplace that self-love was the root of all emotional troubles. It was constituted by voluptuousness, avarice, and ambition. In contrast, man's fulfillment or achievement of "Self" resided in his attainment of "oneness" with a transcendental being. Once separated from this value system, man was nothing. The proposition facing the dramatist was that all facets of purely human personality are equivalent to mere aberration.[10] In its broad outlines, Machado de Assis was to incorporate this Shakespearean vision of character into his art and project a theory of man divided against himself and unable to achieve unity or fulfillment through love.[11] This view is expressed by the narrative process itself in its series of divided narrators—the dead Brás Cubas versus the living character, the emotionally dead D. Casmurro versus the living Bento, Ayres-narrator as opposed to Ayres-character and Ayres the diarist who cannot give what men called love contrasted with Ayres the character who realizes love.

Rubião's division is explicitly drawn in his schism between mind and heart. I have shown the earlier novels in which aspects of this general theory can be found to have constituted a workshop for the last five works. Part of the narrative process is a parody of the reigning schools of literature of which Machado de Assis rejected the realism based on naturalist tenets. Although his own narrative process playfully disrupts illusion at every moment, it achieves its goal of establishing a reality based on esthetic truth. Machado de Assis's experimentalism may thus be viewed as part of his theory of character, in which the note of optimism sounded was equivalent to the artist's achievement of "unity" or fulfillment through the creative act and the example given to the involved, collaborating reader.

NOTES

1. Barreto Filho observes about Dom Casmurro:

> The book is made up of small scenes and incidents in a closed network, very much in obedience to the structure of a play, in the entrances and exits of the characters, in the short dialogues. But it would be a play to which was incorporated the backstage work and the indications of scenic movement. This gives it a unique aspect. It is a new genre, strictly Machadean. [Barreto Filho, op. cit., p. 190]

2. Harvey, op. cit., p. 105.
3. Ibid., p. 124.
4. Ibid., p. 129.
5. Ibid., p. 130.
6. Ibid., p. 137.
7. Ibid., p. 135.
8. Ibid., p. 142.
9. Barroll, op. cit., pp. 46, 47, 49, 253.
10. Ibid., pp. 58, 70, 73.
11. "Machadean characters no longer present a morally unified structure. They are beings divided against themselves without violent struggles in that state where the internal schism enters into decline in commitments and instability of character." Barreto Filho, op. cit., p. 138.

BIBLIOGRAPHY

WORKS OF JOAQUIM MARIA MACHADO DE ASSIS

Obra Completa. 3 vols. Organized by Afrânio Coutinho. Rio de Janeiro: Editora José Aguilar Ltda., 1962.

Vol. 1: *Ressurreição*; *A Mão e a Luva*; *Helena*; *Iáiá Garcia*; *Memórias Póstumas de Brás Cubas*; *Quincas Borba*; *Dom Casmurro*; *Esaú e Jacó*; *Memorial de Aires.*

Vol. 2: *Contos Fluminenses*; *Histórias de Meia-Noite*; *Papéis Avulsos*; *Histórias Sem Data*; *Várias Historias*; *Páginas Recolhidas*; *Relíquias de Casa Velha*; *Outros Contos*; *Tu só, tu, Puro Amor: Não Consultes Médico, Lição de Botânica.*

Vol. 3: *História de Quinze Dias*; *Notas Semanais*; *Balas de Estalo*; *Bons Dias*!; *A Semana*; *Crítica*; *Epistolário.*

CRITICAL WORKS ON MACHADO DE ASSIS

Bagby, Alberto I., Jr. "Fifteen Years of Machado de Assis: A Critical Annotated Bibliography for 1956-74," *Hispania*, Vol. 58 (October 1975), 648-683.

Barbosa, Edgar. "Machado de Assis em alguns dos seus tipos," *Cactus* (Natal), No. 1 (1959), 12-18.

Barreto Filho, José. *Introdução a Machado de Assis.* Rio de Janeiro: Livraria Agir Editora, 1947.

Caldwell, Helen. *The Brazilian Othello of Machado de Assis.* Berkeley and Los Angeles: University of California Press, 1960.

_____. *Machado de Assis, the Brazilian Master and His Novels.* Berkeley, Los Angeles, and London: University of California Press, 1970.

Cândido, Antonio. "Esquema de Machado de Assis." *Vários Escritos.* São Paulo: Livraria Duas Cidades, 1970.

Cardoso, Wilton. *Tempo e memória em Machado de Assis.* Belo Horizonte: Estabelecimentos gráficos Santa Maria, 1958.

Castello, José Aderaldo. *Realidade e Ilusão em Machado de Assis.* São Paulo: Companhia Editora Nacional, 1969.

Chaves, Flávio Loureiro. *O Mundo Social do Quincas Borba.* Porto Alegre: Movimento Instituto Estadual do Livro, 1974.

Corção, Gustavo. *O Desconcerto do Mundo.* Rio de Janeiro: Livraria Agir Editora, 1965.

Coutinho, Afrânio. *A Filosofia de Machado de Assis e Outros Ensaios.* Rio de Janeiro, Vecchi, 1940.

_____. "O Método de Machado de Assis," *Cadernos Brasileiros*, Ano 2, No. 1 (Jan.-Mar. 1960), 20-28.

Dufy, Mary Terese. "Symbolism in *Esaú e Jacó* with Emphasis on Biblical Implication," *Revista de Letras da Faculdade de Filosofia, Ciências e Letras de Assis*, Vol. 5 (1964), 98-116.

Gomes, Eugênio. *As Influências Inglesas de Machado de Assis.* Bahia: 1939.

_____. *Machado de Assis.* Rio de Janeiro: Livraria São José, 1958.

_____. "Quincas Borba," *Cadernos Brasileiros*, Vol. 2, No. 2 (1960), 24-32.

Graça Aranha, José Pereira da. *Machado de Assis e Joaquim Nabuco Comentários e Notas à Correspondência entre estes dois Escritores*, 2nd ed. Rio de Janeiro: F. Briguiet & Cia., 1942.

Grieco, Agrippino. *Machado de Assis*, 2nd ed. Rio de Janeiro, Conquista, 1960.

Jacques, Alfredo. *Machado de Assis, Equívocos da Crítica.* Porto Alegre: Movimento/IEI, 1974.

MacAdam, Alfred J. "Rereading *Ressurreição*," *Luso-Brazilian Review*, Vol. 9, No. 2 (Winter 1972), 47-57.

Magalhães, Raymundo, Jr. *Ao Redor de Machado de Assis.* Rio de Janeiro: Editora Civilização Brasileira, S.A., 1958.

_____. *Machado de Assis Desconhecido*, 3rd ed. Rio de Janeiro: Editora Civilização Brasileira, S.A., 1957.

Massa, Jean-Michel. *A Juventude de Machado de Assis.* Translated by Marco Aurelio de Moura Matos. Rio de Janeiro: Civilização Brasileira, 1971.

Matos, Mario. *Machado de Assis: O Homem e a Obra.* São Paulo: Companhia Editora Nacional, 1939.

Mattosa Camara, J., Jr. *Ensaios Machadianos.* Rio de Janeiro: Livraria Acadêmica, 1962.

Maya, Alcides. *Machado de Assis (algumas notas sobre o "humour"),* 2nd ed. Rio de Janeiro: Publicações da Academia Brasileira, 1942.

Meyer, Augusto. *Machado de Assis.* Rio de Janeiro: Livraria São José, 1958.

Moisés, Massaud. "Machado de Assis e o Realismo," *Anhembia* (São Paulo), Vol. 35, No. 105 (Agosto 1959), 469-479.

_____. *Temas Brasileiros.* São Paulo: Conselho Estadual de Cultura, Comissão, V, 142 de Literatura, 1964.

Monteiro, Ivan C., and Estrella, Hairton M. *Metalinguagem em "Quincas Borba" de Machado de Assis.* Rio de Janeiro: Livraria Academica, 1973.

Montello, Josué. *O Presidente Machado de Assis.* São Paulo: Livraria Martins Editora, 1961.

Nunes, Maria Luisa. "Machado de Assis's Theory of the Novel," *Latin American Literary Review,* Vol. 4, No. 7 (Fall-Winter 1975), 57-66.

Oliveira Lima, M. de. *Machado de Assis Son Oeuvre Littéraire.* Paris: Librairie Garnier Frères, 1917.

Pacheco, João. *O Realismo* (1870-1900). São Paulo: Editora Cultrix, 1963.

Pati, Francisco. *Dicionário de Machado de Assis História e biografia dos personagens.* São Paulo: Rede Latina Editora Ltda., 1958.

Pereira, Astrojildo. *Machado de Assis.* Rio de Janeiro: Livraria São José, 1959.

Pereira, Lucia Miguel. *Machado de Assis Estudo Crítico e Bográfico.* 5th ed. Rio de Janeiro: José Olympio, 1955.

Pólvora, Hélio. "Preface" to Joaquim Maria Machado de Assis, *Helena.* Rio de Janeiro: MEC-Civilização Brasileira, 1975.

Pontes, Eloy. *A Vida Contradictória de Machado de Assis.* Rio de Janeiro: Livraria José Olympio, 1939.

Pujol, Alfredo. *Machado de Assis,* 2nd ed. Rio de Janeiro: Livraria José Olympio, 1934.

Rabello, Sylvio. *Caminhos da Província.* Recife: Impresa Universitaria da Universidade do Recife, 1965.

Riedel, Dirce Cortes. *Metáfora, o Espelho de Machado de Assis.* Rio de Janeiro: Livraria Francisco Alves Editora, S.A., 1974.

_____. *O Tempo no Romance Machadeano.* Rio de Janeiro: Livraria São José, 1959.

Romero, Sylvio. *Machado de Assis,* 2nd ed. Rio de Janeiro: Livraria José Olympio, 1936.

Santiago, Silviano. "Ode, conto e romance: Machado de Assis 1872," *Suplemento Literário do Estado de São Paulo,* January 4, 1969, January 18, 1969, May 31, 1969.

_____. "Retórica da Verossimilhança," *Cadernos da Puc* (Rio de Janeiro), No. 11 (October 1972), 1-18.

Schwarz, Roberto. *Ao Vencedor as Batatas*. São Paulo: Duas Cidades, 1977.

Soares, Maria Nazaré Lins. *Machado de Assis e a Análise da Expressão*. Rio de Janeiro: Instituto Nacional do Livro, 1968.

Sousa, J. Galante de. *Bibliografia de Machado de Assis*. Rio de Janeiro: Instituto Nacional do Livro, 1955.

Veríssimo, José. *História da Literatura Brasileira*, 3rd ed. Rio de Janeiro: Livraria José Olympio, 1954.

Viana Filho, Luiz. *A Vida de Machado de Assis*. São Paulo: Livraria Martins Editora, 1965.

Virgillo, Carmelo, ed. *Correspondência de Machado de Assis com Magalhães de Azeredo*. Rio de Janeiro: Instituto Nacional do Livro, 1969.

OTHER CRITICAL WORKS

Aristotle. *Poetics*. Translated by Gerald F. Else. Ann Arbor: Ann Arbor Paperbacks, The University of Michigan Press, 1970.

Auerbach, Erich. *Mimesis*. Translated by Willard R. Trask. Princeton: Princeton University Press, 1968.

Barroll, J. Leeds. *Artificial Persons*. Columbia, S.C.: University of South Carolina Press, 1974.

Bayley, John. *The Characters of Love*. London: Constable, 1960.

Booth, Wayne. *The Rhetoric of Fiction*. Chicago and London: The University of Chicago Press, 1961.

Ducrot, Oswald, and Todorov, Tzvetan. *Dictionnaire Encyclopédique des Sciences du Langage*. Paris: Editions du Seuil, 1972.

Ducrot, Oswald: Todorov, Tzvetan; Sperber, Dan; Safouan, Moustafa; and Wahl, François. *Qu'est-ce que le Structuralisme*. Paris: Editions du Seuil, 1968.

Forster, E. M. *Aspects of the Novel*. New York: A Harvest Book, Harcourt, Brace and World, Inc., 1954.

Frye, Northrop. *Anatomy of Criticism*. Princeton: Princeton University Press, 1957.

Galsworthy, J. *The Creation of Character in Literature*. Oxford: Clarendon Press, 1931.

Gass, William H. *Fiction and the Figures of Life*. New York: Alfred A. Knopf, 1970.

Genette, Gérard. *Figures III*. Paris: Editions du Seuil, 1972.

Harvey, W. J. *Character and the Novel*. London: Chatto and Windus, 1970.

Iser, Wolfgang. *The Implied Reader*. Baltimore and London: The Johns Hopkins University Press, 1975.

James, Henry. *The Art of Fiction*. Boston: Charles Upham and Co., 1884.

———. *The Art of the Novel*. New York and London: Charles Scribner's Sons, 1962.

Kayser, Wolfgang. "Qui Raconte le Roman?" *Poétique*, Vol. 4 (1970), 498-510.

Liddell, Robert. *Robert Liddell on the Novel*. Chicago: the University of Chicago Press, 1969.

Lubbock, Percy. *The Craft of Fiction*. New York: The Viking Press, 1968.

Mauriac, François. *Le Romancier et ses Pesonnages*. Paris: Editions R. A. Corrêa, 1933.

Mendilow, A. A. *Time and the Novel*. London: Peter Nevill, 1952.

Meyerhoff, Hans. *Time in Literature*. Berkeley and Los Angeles: University of California Press, 1955.

Muir, Edwin. *The Structure of the Novel*. London: The Hogarth Press, 1967.

New Literary History. "Changing Views of Character," Vol. V, No. 2 (Winter 1974).

Ortega y Gassett. *The Dehumanization of Art*. Translated by Willard Trask. Garden City, N.Y.: Doubleday and Co., Inc., 1956.

Pouillon, J. *Temps et Roman*. Paris: Gallimard, 1946.

Poulet, Georges. *Studies in Human Time*. Translated by Elliott Coleman. Baltimore: The Johns Hopkins Press, 1956.

Price, Martin. "People of the Book: Character in Forster's *A Passage to India*," *Critical Inquiry*, Vol. 1, No. 3 (March 1975).

———. "The Logic of Intensity: More on Character," *Critical Inquiry*, Vol. 2, No. 2 (Winter 1975).

———. "The Other Self: Thoughts about Character in the Novel," in *Imagined Worlds: Essays on Some English Novels and Novelists in Honor of John Butt*. Edited by Maynard Mack and Ian Gregor. London: Methuen and Co., 1968.

Prince, Gerald. "Introduction à l'Étude du Narrataire." *Poétique*, Vol. 14, Paris: Editions du Seuil, 1973.

Reis, Carlos. Estatuto e Perspectivas do Narrador na Ficcao de Eca de Queiros. Coimbra: Livraria Almedina, 1975.

Sartre, J. P. "M. François Mauriac et la Liberté" in *Situations I*. Paris: Gallimard, 1968, pp. 33-52.

Scholes, Robert, and Kellogg, Robert. *The Nature of Narrative*. London, Oxford, and New York: Oxford University Press, 1971.

Stevick, Philip, ed. *The Theory of the Novel*. New York: The Free Press, 1967.

Swinden, Patrick. *Unofficial Selves: Character in the Novel from Dickens to the Present Day*. London: Macmillan, 1973.

Todorov, Tzvetan. *Poétique de la Prose*. Paris: Editions du Seuil, 1971.

Tomachevski, B. "Thématique," in *Théorie de la Littérature*. Paris: Editions du Seuil, 1965.

Wellek, René. *Concepts of Criticism*. New Haven and London: Yale University Press, 1963.

Wellek, René and Warren, Austin. *Theory of Literature*, 3rd ed. New York: A Harvest Book, Harcourt, Brace and World, Inc., 1956.

Wilson, Rawdon. "On Character: A Reply to Martin Price," *Critical Inquiry*, Vol. 2, No. 1 (Autumn 1975).

INDEX

About the Author

MARIA LUISA NUNES is Associate Professor of Portuguese at the University of Pittsburgh. Her earlier works include *Lima Barreto* and *Portuguese Colonial in America*.

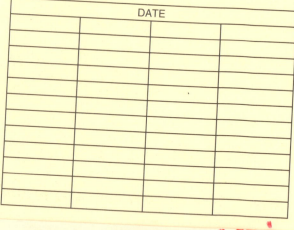